BITS AND PIECES
An Autobiography

© 2017 by Albin Seth Conkey

Albin Seth Conkey

BITS AND PIECES
An Autobiography

To my mother, Irene Lillian Avery, whom I only knew for 15 short years but who still visits me in my dreams.

Special thanks to my daughter, Victoria, who tirelessly helped me complete this project.

PREFACE

I started to document some of my life events here many years ago. I wrote a few pages and had to quit for one reason or another, only to find myself encouraged to do more. I do not know if it was someone or something or possibly the idea of finishing something, but now that my children are all adults they constantly encourage me to work on it.

I am not a writer. That is a different thing. It is difficult for me to compose some of what I have lived and explain the affect it has had on my life, but one day in Florida, perhaps twenty years ago, I started to pen some notes of interesting events that I could retell without offending anyone. These recollections are but a few of the hundreds (perhaps thousands) of stories which became events that have helped to mold my life into the one I enjoy today.

Here are my bits and pieces of the "good old days" which just may resonate with you as they are shared once again.

Standing here my eyes trace the northern landscape as I ponder the past. The view is splendid, so splendid that I remember countless city artists taking up their palettes in attempts to capture the colors and beauty of this isolated town in the foot hills of the White Mountains. This is Ellsworth, New Hampshire, my home.

My eyes continue to search for something to confirm, or in some way testify to the dreams of my past. I can see the old homestead in the distance, a washed-out white clapboard New England style house in desperate need of attention. It's fields and yard now so overgrown that the panoramic views it once offered have surrendered to the overgrowth of brush and trees. The terrain has changed as well. I temporarily struggle to get my bearings and realize soil has been borrowed for new construction around the neighboring Stinson Lake. I fall deeper into reminiscing about all those things that made me feel like my life in the White Mountains of New Hampshire was more than just ordinary.

My family tree traces back to the early 1800's to Ronald, Michigan, near Woodard Lake where Albert S. Conkey, my paternal grandfather, lived with his brother, George, father, Eli and mother, Amanda.

Albert S. Conkey stood over six feet with white hair, which he always combed. He was well built and sported a large mustache on an attractive face. Every Sunday, whether he was going somewhere or not, he dressed up like a business man. From his childhood, Albert S. worked the large farm there at Woodard Lake with his family. He was a favored son and was able to become a world traveler, even participating in the

Alaskan Gold Rush. On that venture he not only found gold, but he returned with a tusk from a Wooly Mammoth which was later cut and used to make many items including a cribbage board which remained at our home for years.

In 1912, Albert S. was invited to a card game in Shilo, Michigan where he reportedly won the farm in Ellsworth, New Hampshire.

While in Shilo, he met a young school teacher named Olive Heath with whom he became romantically involved. They were soon married and embarked on an adventure which would take them by train and horse drawn sleigh from the small town of Shilo to the foothills of the White Mountains. Their home would be that newly won property in Ellsworth, New Hampshire.

Ellsworth, in earlier years was a bustling town of small farms, country stores, mills, a creamery, schools, a meeting house, churches, boarding houses and trade shops.

They rode over the hill and into the valley where they could see a white clapboard farm house and a large barn. The yard had a circular drive and could be entered both from the south and the north. There was a large butternut tree to the south of the house, large sugar maples in front, smaller fruit trees, and berry and current bushes on the north side. Inside it was the typical old farm house; well maintained, with wood floors, decorative floral design papered walls and plastered ceilings. In the kitchen a large wood range with warming ovens and a water reservoir stood. Under a window on the west side of the room was a large cast iron sink with a wood barrel for water. On the north side of the house was a parlor with a large pot bellied stove and a wood box. The farm had out-buildings to house a two-hole toilet, barns for horses and cattle, chicken coops and the big saw mill.

Somehow they made it through the first winter with little help. Grandpa was a hard working farmer, but he now found himself in a location that was not farm friendly. Winters were harsh and long and the terrain and soils were not good.

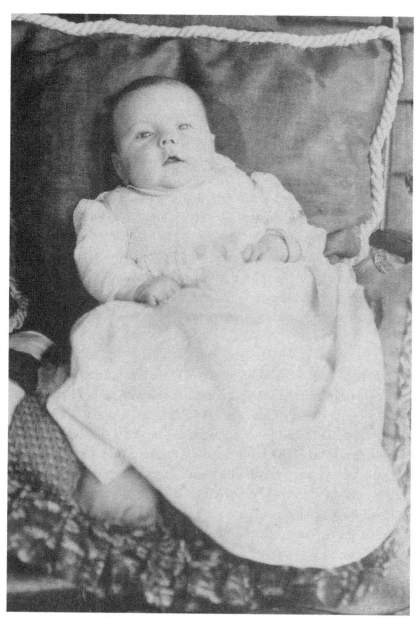

My father, Albert Russell Conkey.

My grandparents were doing what they could to hold onto the farm by growing produce and hay to sell to anyone that would buy. They both did odd jobs. Grandpa sold farm goods, lumber and gravel as well as work on town roads. Grandma Olive did the house work, rented rooms from time to time and was a teacher at one of Ellsworth's two Elementary Schools. She gave birth to a son in August of 1912 (Albert George) who died four days later, a daughter (Florida) in 1913, another daughter (Emaline) in 1914, a Daughter (Maud) in 1915, and my father (Albert Russell) in 1916.

She continued to work that fall, doing her best to keep the house in order even though she was ill with an infection from child birth. Grandpa got a message to Dr. Elwin Ladd in Wentworth and he made a house call. By the time Dr. Ladd attended to Olive it was too late as she had suffered from peripheral nephritis. On November 6th, 1920 and at the young age of only 36, Olive ended the suffering from infection which she had endured for three months.

***

Grandpa was very set back by the loss of Olive and not able to properly care for his four children. He had corresponded with his brother George and George's wife, Myrtle, in Michigan about possible help. George and Myrtle came to Ellsworth and took Emaline and Maud home with them.

Florida and Dad stayed with Grandpa for some time. Grandpa struggled for three years trying to make ends meet and care for the two remaining children. He had employed house help but remained depressed and Dad was placed in an orphanage in Franklin, New Hampshire. Dad stayed at the orphanage for some time and Florida was fostered to a friend's home.

Dad returned home after a few years and lived with Grandpa. He helped with chores and attended school in the local Ellsworth Elementary School.

At 18 years of age, Dad (nicknamed Bud) was a handsome and charming young man. He had visited a friend in Thornton where he met a young girl of fifteen, Irene Avery, as well as her sister Viola and brother Clarence. They partied at Blake Mountain where they ran in the snow and went sledding on the hills owned by Irene's grandmother. They stayed there at the Guy Downing farm for a few weeks. Dad was very cocky and had a few disagreements with other young men over his new friend, Irene. Herman Rietsma was a neighbor that lived down the road a piece and he was not at all happy over the idea of Dad moving in on his territory. He was sweet on Viola, Irene's sister. Later on Herman married Viola. She died from infection after giving birth to a stillborn.

After a spell, Dad returned to Ellsworth to work with his father. He was a wild teenager and his father was an enabler, giving him cars and whatever he wanted.

From the front porch where Albert would be seen sitting in an old porch rocker, from time to time, people passing by would stop to talk. It seemed to be the custom to stop and share news and discuss politics. Dad and Grandpa were always active in town business.

***

It was an early spring day and Grandpa heard a car drive in.

Guy Downing had stopped by to inform Dad that Irene was eager to see him. Dad was suspicions at the time and decided to go visit his sisters in Michigan. This proved to be a fast trip; his sister Emaline and new husband Gerald had already learned the news of Irene's pregnancy. He would soon get things set straight by Emaline. "You get your butt back there and do right by that girl and your child." It was spring now and Dad returned to Thornton to see his pregnant friend. Dad spent time with her and other girlfriends, but soon he married Irene. They lived at Guy Downing's Farm until Albert Junior was born in November of 1935.

They then moved to Ellsworth where Grandpa was in need of help. It was after Thanksgiving, the weather was cold and preparing firewood was more than Grandpa could do.

A brown-pillowed Morris chair was set near the potbellied stove and there he would sit dressed like a wealthy business man. He played

My mother, Irene, with Albert Junior.

cards and would read night and day and later tell stories influenced by those readings including the world news.

Irene lived with Dad and Grandpa, doing the bulk of the work to run the place and prepare meals. She gave birth to Maxine in August of 1937 and was pregnant with me in early 1938.

Because the CCC camps in the three ponds area were finishing and closing, hundreds of loggers and workers that supported the local area were moving to find employment. The year of 1938 was not a typical year. Everyone was suffering due to a bad economy, lack of jobs and money caused by the depression that President Roosevelt had tried to end for more than five years.

There was little communication other than radio (if the battery had not run down) and the local newspaper in Plymouth. A lot of communication was passed on by visiting neighbors. The weather had been rainy for days. To look out from the porch, all the surrounding mountains were blanketed with leaves as though freshly painted with bright colors from an artist's palette. Still wet, but brilliant in the morning light. They were getting ready for the frosts and winds of October to send them into their new season.

The weather changed without any warning or tell tale clues. The rain became very forceful and was pushed with a wind of well over 100 miles per hour. The next day, to stand on the front porch and look out at the surrounding mountains, they appeared naked and gray. Trees were leafless and damaged by the high winds. This was the great hurricane of the Northeast. This storm had created downed trees, wash outs and excessive road damage. It was the worst storm in recorded history to strike New England with hundreds killed and millions of dollars in damage. The bright side was, the hurricane was the beginning of the end of a depression that had crippled the country for many years.

Dad had been working for the New Hampshire state highway maintenance department for over three years. With the destruction by the storm, he was guaranteed a job for some time.

Dad had an old Reo dump truck which he used to truck dirt from pits on the farm, to repair roads, lumber and materials for bridges while working for the highway department. He would leave early in the morning and come home late. He was trying to pay the bills for his wife, two children and his ailing father.

***

It was now the 27th of October and nights were already quite cold. The house was being heated by a wood kitchen range plus a big pot bellied stove in the parlor room. In the task of carrying the night's wood, Irene had broken her water and before dawn on October 28th, I became the next son of the Conkey family. Mom delivered me with a little help from Dad. Because there was no electric power or gas lamps, the house was not very light. An old oil lamp was the only source of light. In spite of all adverse conditions, everything turned out fine. The next day Dad did not go to work. The farm chores and helping around the house had taken him too long. That afternoon he took his rusty old Reo and went to recruit Irene's mother, Margaret Avery, to help with the house work so that he would be able to go back to work.

In the next year things were not going well. Grandpa was suffering from a severe prostate problem and his health was failing. The mill was not running, most of the farm animals and equipment had to be sold to pay mounting debts.

As a small 3 year old I was happy in my surroundings blond (or toe headed) and running around the farm with my 6 year old brother Albert Jr., my older sister Maxine and now a 2 year old sister Sylvia.

Grammy Avery would come and stay for a while after each child was born and was there helping before the birth of George.

***

It was early summer and there was a lot going on. In all the excitement Grandpa had moved from his old Morris chair to the privacy of his

My mother, Irene (20), Albert (5), Maxine (4), me (2) and Sylvia (under 1)

bedroom. He was still having severe health issues and was attended by Dr. Harold Palmer frequently to comfort him. At the age of 70 and in the morning of November 6th, 1940 Grandpa was gone.

Dad drove to Stinson lake to send a telegram informing relatives and to summon Dr. Palmer. I was so very young at the time, my memory is a little fuzzy, but I do remember my grandfather, what he looked like, his manner and how he treated me.

I was not old enough to grasp the meaning of death, so I did not mourn as others did. Aunt Emaline and Aunt Maud had come from Michigan and just so many other people: friends, relatives, past employees and neighbors.

The old wood kitchen range was so warm and the smell of the doughnut kettle of hot fat with a colander of hot donuts draining was a sure fine lure to attract everyone there. Grammy sure could make good donuts.

At the funeral, or soon after, while my Aunt Emaline was still there, there was conversation with my mother and father about taking me home with them. They only had one daughter and hundreds of acres to farm. They would listen to my 3 year old chatter ("I have a pocket, you have a pocket") and be captivated by my presence. My Dad was not ready to let anyone go at that time.

As time went on, Dad had written letters to Emaline and Maud about the status of the farm with all the debts and need of maintenance and it was decided that the farm would have to be sold to pay debts and share any inheritance with his sisters.

Dad had purchased a small tract of land just south of the old farm where Dad and friends had been working for some time.

In preparation, he and Mom's brother Clarence built a small log house on a knoll there. They cut and pealed logs, trucked boards and appropriated all the items to assemble a primitive home for his fast growing family. The construction took some time as Dad was working a full time job and he only bartered with friends to help in their spare time. Mom was busy packing oakum, old rope, and rags in the cracks between the logs. She then mixed a cement and plaster mud to trowel over it. Dad, Clarence and friends worked on the roof. They put fiber board on the ceilings and walls upstairs.

With pick and shovels they dug a cellar and laid large fieldstone walls to hold the dirt back and support the house. The cellar was small but it held hundreds of jars of vegetables, jellies, crocks of pork, pickles, and barrels of cider. Also, there was a bin to store potatoes, cabbage, turnip, and many other items could be found there from time to time.

Dad had built a barn for a cow and a few odd farm animals; pigs, rabbits, sheep, calves or whatever he might find while frequently going to auctions.

Dad was always able to get drinking buddies and other people to help get the house built and everything done. As a result, everything was substandard and the craftsmanship was primitive.

We all moved into that partially finished log house that spring. The gardens and outside work were well under way. We were stocking the cellar with food for the winter. It was already early fall. Dad was working on the state road. He was bringing home firewood everyday to prepare for the winter ahead.

On September 1st of 1941, Mom, now 22 years old, delivered her 5th baby. George, named after Uncle George in Michigan, Chester for Mom's father. He was a large baby, weighing over nine pounds. He was the apple of Dad's eye from day one. He was also the first one to be born in the new home.

***

The old homestead was sold to a very nice wealthy family from Long Island, New York. They repaired the house back to it's original condition. They hired workers that removed all of the barns, out buildings, sawmill and sheds. The old wooden front porch was replaced with a stone and concrete one. The clapboards were replaced and painted. The house looked great for years.

The Rienfelts seemed to always have the personality and treats that were irresistible to me and my brothers and sisters. They used the place as a second home or vacation house and were not there very often. We would watch for their car and walk down to see them whenever we could. They always brought their house maid/cook with them. She made great treats and was very generous.

Like his father, Dad loved to tell stories, but he did not have all the adventures that his father had yet. Dinner or supper time meals were a good time to see what was on everyone's mind.

Albert had started school in the fall of 1942. He walked to Rosco Dunkley's where Horace Patterson picked him up every morning and dropped him off after school everyday. No phone or communication, just a planned rendezvous. Everyone was always on time.

In the spring of 1942 we planted our gardens and restocked the cellar as always. Living from the land and enjoying what little time we got between chores by exploring the fields and woods around the small farm. I was only 4 and Albert 7 but we were making fish poles from saplings and trying to catch trout in the streams near the house. House chores became more intense as time went on with the churning of butter and carrying wood and water. We fed the animals and weeded the garden under Mom's guidance. Mom was pregnant with brother Art now. Dad was still working on the roads and talking politics, war and the news. On February 28th, 1943 Art joined the family in the middle of a cold night. Of all the children in our family, there did not seem to be any obvious health issues so far. However, Mom was concerned a lot about Art, he was weak and did not walk or stand much as a toddler.

Albert and I were making sap spouts from ash shoots, cutting one half inch diameter pieces approximately four inches long. We then heated a length of wire to burn a hole through the soft hart, then drilled a hole into every maple tree that we could find. And in that hole we drove our newly made spout under it, we drove a nail where we hung lard buckets, washed oil cans and any other vessel at our disposal. It was a slow process collecting the sap, carrying it to the house and storing for evaporating. Mom had a square sap pan on the kitchen stove and it was boiling fiercely, the steam filled the house with a sweet aroma,

Dad had befriended a journalist, Mrs. Roberts, a middle-aged robust pleasant lady that worked at the Plymouth Record. If there was anything newsworthy, Mrs. Roberts was there with her camera. We could often be seen in local papers sporting our rag clothes and things of interest at the time, such as big fish or pussy willows.

gathering and running down the windows. When it was all done, there would be a supply of syrup to sweeten and flavor a lot of Mom's cooking.

Mom and Grammy were always patching clothes and making sheets from bags that were saved from grain, sugar or flower. Scraps were cut for diapers.

Another season had passed the planting and harvesting went on as usual and Maxine had joined Albert on the walk to school.

Now Mom was pregnant with Raymond. Already with six children, two in diapers, and one barely potty trained, my mother was doing laundry, preparing meals and all the house work.

Raymond was born January 28, 1944 and now there were seven children and mom was only 25 years old.

It was March 1944 and as supervisor of the check list, Dad would hook the work horse to a sled and bundle every one up in what warm clothes that could be found. We would walk and ride to the town meeting, where he and Mom would vote and visit while Dad did his job. Then we would climb onto the sled and the horse's back for that four miles back. It was a long trek. We went up steep snow covered hills by the Murphy farm, down hills and around corners over brooks and bridges. The landscape was a winter wonderland with snow sparkling and hanging from the evergreens. It was cold but there was not much complaining about it. Everyone was so active or bundled together on the sled that we stayed warm on the way home. Dad and Mom were having conversations about town matters and the war. A lot of chit chat, crying babies and a stop at Charlie Sergeant's house made the trip seem much faster.

Dad had decided that he was going to join the army and he discussed plans to move Mom and the children to West Campton for the time that he would be gone.

We had moved the provisions from the cellar and our necessities in to the back of Dad's old truck and were on our way to what was supposed to be a better home for the next winter. In West Campton we were on a black top road and close to neighbor friends of Dad's. Dad just seemed to disappear one night and Mom and brother Albert (8), Maxine (6), me (5), Sylvia (4), George (2) and Art not yet 1, were left to fare for ourselves.

Art was frail and had the rickets. A neighbor, Mabel Jackson, would come to help Mom and provide him with supplements.

The house was a small two-room camp (just a tar paper shack) with a lean-to on the backside. No electricity, no inside walls, no insulation, no plumbing, make shift windows and a small wood stove. The camp was wrapped with black paper and had three single pane windows.

There was a small shed built on the back which housed the cow and a little hay. Additional hay was carried from the dairy farm across the road. Water came from a dug spring which froze solid after a couple months. The winter was long and hard. Some days Mom would drag logs into the shack to cut them to put them into the stove to heat and cook with. She would melt snow for water on the stove in a large galvanized tub that everyone took turns bathing in. Then she would boil that water in an old copper boiler to clean our clothes, then boil the make-shift diapers stirring them back and forth with a clothes stick, all with the same water.

MANCHESTER, N. H. THURSDAY, MARCH 16, 1944

ELLSWORTH FATHER OF SEVEN TO ENTER SERVICE

Albert Conkey, 28, Ellsworth father of seven children, who shortly will enter the service, is shown above with his family. Conkey, supervisor of the checklist in Ellsworth, Tuesday was on duty at the annual town meeting. Left to right: Maxime, 6; Albert, Jr., 8; Mrs. Conkey with month-old baby, Raymond; Conkey himself holding Arthur, 1 year; while seated on sled in front, are Sylvia, 4, George, 2, and Albin, 5.

Mrs. Roberts believed this to be of interest in the paper, so she met at the log house in Ellsworth to photograph the family a few days before Dad left.

Over the bed and between Betsy's shed and our sleeping area was a window. On those ever so frequent cold mornings when the fire had gone out, we would encourage Betsy to stick her head in that window and breath her hot steamy breath over our bed which we all slept in.

Maxine and Albert were going to school in West Campton. They road with Mildred Avery. She lived across the road and was the school teacher, as well as the owner of the dairy farm.

Mildred had a small family; a daughter Mary Lou, and two sons Bill and Harold Junior, named after her husband. They were a family that Dad was friends with and believed they would aid Mom in time of need while he was away.

One sunny winter day, the snow was melting and the camp was leaking a lot and Albert was helping Mom chop ice off the roof with an old axe. The head was loose on the handle and would keep coming off. While things seemed to be going well with the removal of large chunks of ice, that loose head flew off and hit my brother George in the head. Mom grabbed him up and away she ran to the neighbors. Albert and the rest of us stayed home doing the things that seemed helpful until Mom returned that evening with George and his bandages. Even though he had a cut, it was a glancing blow so it was not very deep.

Mom was under pressure to get out of this shack. Mom's father, Chester Avery (Grandpa) came to our house to tell us about another camp just up the hill from where they lived which we could move into.

Before the spring we were moved by Grandpa and friends to a better location down the road a couple of miles. The house had a separate bedroom and Mom always hung fabric to make privacy for beds. There was a good yard, good neighbors and a good trout brook just down the hill. Grammy and Grandpa were next door neighbors and they were helping us any way they could.

Mom took a job at Doles Mill at the Campton Dam and was making socks for the Army. She was struggling to keep food on the table and pay bills. Betsy was in an old barn down at Turkey Jim's where mom and Grandpa shared a garden. Albert and I would walk the roads picking up returnable bottles to turn in at Avery's General Store to help with the family food bill. Old Will Avery was so compassionate and sympathetic to our family and he let us run a bill for necessities without any limits as far as I knew. He sold grain for Betsy, food and hardware and delivered most always.

It was your patriotic duty to do what one could to support the efforts of our military. We collected tin cans and flattened them for a program to recycle for the military. We picked milkweed blossoms for a silk experiment for parachutes and wrote to Dad as much as possible.

Many food products and necessities such as sugar, meat, petroleum products and other items were rationed and hard to buy. We did have some ration stamps and tokens but did not have much money.

There was a small post office in Avery's general store and Mom would eagerly run in there after work to check the mail. She was always looking for some word from Dad. After many days of disappointment, a little letter came. They were always censored by the government to make sure that no important information could be gained by reading the contents. After picking up a bag of sugar and a couple of bottles of Certo (a fruit pectin) she always thanked Will for his generosity as she left the store and ran home. Grammy was caring for us children and preparing to make blackberry jam. The berries had recently been picked across the road and had to be used soon as there was no refrigeration other than a small ice box.

Mom made a pen one day to hold a pig she got with Grandpa. She fed it everything she could find, from table scraps to wild apples, grain or whatever. She had purchased a new ax from Will Avery and was attempting to cut a rock maple tree to make another fence post for the pig pen.

The ax struck the rock maple tree and it glanced off to end up in the muscle of her leg. She was bleeding badly and ran uphill to the Jackson house where she passed out and fell in front of their kitchen sink. I never did hear how her leg was cared for but I know she had a hideous scar for the rest of her life.

The camp was not exactly cozy but Mom and us had done all we could to make this a warmer and more comfortable place to live while Dad was giving all his efforts to the War. We packed the cracks with paper or rag scraps to keep the snow and wind out. Mom mixed up paste from flour and water and covered the board walls with a heavy printed-paper. She covered the rags and paper packing with the flour paste. This worked miracles to create a cleaner and much warmer house than we had before.

There was always a shortage of meat during the war and nothing was safe around our home. Mom had a talent for creating a good meal with most all animals. A shed built on to the house to hold firewood had a window hinged from the top which one could lift up and hook with a hook and eye. This would allow someone to throw wood into the shed for storage after it had been split and prepared for the stove. The shed housed shovels, rakes, hoes, and a dung fork and other tools used in running the house and maintaining the barn for Betsy. It would hold a deer carcass or whatever Mom and her Dad might get for us to live on for meat. Mom was an avid hunter and an excellent marks person.

One cold winter day there was a large deer carcass hanging in the shed. The wood was neatly stacked on all the walls and up to the window, which had been left open, hooked with the hook and eye. This shed also served as a walk-in cooler, a mud room or entrance to the house, and one would enter the shed through a door, then up a couple of steps then through a door into the kitchen/living room of the house. There were tools hanging and leaning against the wall beside the door and the deer was hanging from the center of the shed where it had been skinned, washed and left to cure. After shoveling the drive from newly fallen snow and eating our supper of deer liver and onions, everyone had gone to bed and was fast asleep.

During the quiet night hours, a half starved bobcat found the smell of the fresh venison hanging in the shed. The bobcat managed to find that open window and jump up and through it. He then climbed down the wood to have a feast on Mom's deer. After gorging on the meat, he tried to scale the woodpile to get back out the window. The woodpile fell to a loud clatter that brought Mom off her bed and out the door in a couple of leaps. What this bobcat did not know was that the State of New Hampshire had a bounty on him for just trying to live. Fifty dollars was just a lot of money in those days. The job at Dole's Mill was paying less than one dollar an hour then. Mom was not about to let this windfall get away without some attempt to cash in. She opened the door to the shed and in the faint morning light caught a glimpse of the culprit that had caused such a noise. That bobcat and Mom knew the race was on for the window. Mom in her long nightgown with her hair down and bare feet. She snatched up the dung fork by the door and swung it in a circle high around the ceiling. She managed to hit the hook and knock it out of the eye allowing the window to drop closed. Now it was Mom with her dung fork and that big old wild cat in one room together. Even though Mom had closed the door going into the house to prevent the cat from getting by her, my brothers and sisters and I could hear every sound in this battle for survival. Believe me, there is not a more blood curdling sound than a bobcat taking a dung fork to death. We were so happy to see Mom come back through that door.

After the clean up and dressing for the day, Mom got us all off to that little one room school about a half mile down the road.

West Campton was a busy little village back then and we had to walk to school each day down the big hill by Grammy and Grandpa's with Arthur Moulton's shingle mill on the brook across the street, the home of Ralph and Hilda Avery, the middle aged son of Will Avery, the big general store and post office and the maple lodge across the street which was the home of a school mate, Arthur Bowles. There were other homes in the area but not significant at the time.

That bobcat incident was typical of Mom, however it was found newsworthy enough to print in the Plymouth Record, a local paper published about six miles away. Grandpa and Mom were in the paper holding up the bobcat and Mom got her check for fifty dollars from the Fish and Game Department.

I couldn't find the picture of my mother with the bobcat she found in the shed, but here's a picture of Grandpa with a small bobcat at about the same time.

During World War II, all communication between service men and their families were censored by the government to prevent any security sensitive information from be gained by reading these letters. That first winter went by with a few of those censored letters with the black spots which covered words or phrases that may have been questionable to the one doing the censoring at that time. The letters were reduced in size and the print was small also. A sentence could be printed with a couple of the words or its entire subject blacked out. Mom read and reread them so frequently that she would memorize their contents word for word. Always trying to understand what was blacked out.

Then there was a notice of missing in action somewhere in Belgium or France. Later we got word Dad had been seriously injured and left for a period in a foxhole where he was rescued and hospitalized. After he was released from medical care he was back with his infantry group. As time went on with the war, he found himself in many heroic and life threatening situations. One day Mom got a telegram that broke her up to an extent I had never seen before. Between the sobs she told us that Dad had been wounded in battle and was not expected to live. He was hospitalized in Europe and Mom began to receive those letters again. Neighboring women with husbands in the war and with similar problems would stop by and console Mom. There seemed to be a lot of people that were injured or killed at that time. They compared letters and organized to help each other.

Mom was still working for the Doles at the mill making socks. She also shared a garden at Turkey Jim's where she milked the cow on the way to work and on the way home every day.

Dad recovered from his injuries enough to be transferred to a hospital in Oklahoma. In that hospital he was treated for broken ear drums. He was still suffering from severe psychological problems brought on by the war. He served as a point man with Company G., 117th Infantry, Old Hickory Division where he was constantly subjected to some of the worst experiences of the war. He had just finished digging a fox hole for shelter when a German grenade exploded on the top rim of his hole.

The explosion was close and very loud. Dad had lost consciousness right away. As Dad laid in the bottom of his fox hole bleeding from deep cuts and internal injuries, the battle was going on all around him. An army medic found him and he was taken to a medic center where he received blood transfusions and emergency surgery to stabilize him. Shrapnel from the grenade had entered his neck and face, removing some back teeth and cutting his neck. The concussion from the explosion had broken his ear drums and created other damage to his head.

All I knew was, all of us kids missed him and felt like Mom. We just wanted him home. One mid summer day, Albert and I had been fishing in the nearby brook at the shingle mill. We fished every time we could, mostly for the fun of it. However, we were a good provider of the food supply to the family. We had just cleaned up the catch and a taxi pulled up the drive. Out stepped my father in his crisp starched Army uniform. He was decorated with many medals for heroism, marksmanship and many other things. The reunion was overwhelming; Dad and Mom seemed so happy. It was a hot summer day and we all partied outside in the yard.

One afternoon the skies had darkened. There was a large thunder head that dropped mothball size hale. All of us kids were scooping up the hale in an old washbasin to make a pile to see how long it would last before melting away. When the thunder and lightening had stopped we realized there was a commotion in the front side of the house. Dad was experiencing delusions of war combat and attempting to dig a foxhole in the front yard with his bare hands. He was scared out of his mind. Even though he could not hear, the vibration from the storm mimicked explosions in his mind.

Dad suffered with mental problems from horror of war and fatigue. Because of his hearing loss, he was taught to read lips and in his outbursts of war fits, we could not talk to him. The next few months were real trials for everyone. Dad drank, partied with old friends and tried to get his life in order.

Mom and Dad reunited.

Dad was out one evening, visiting with Phonny Downing, a road contractor friend. Phonny was in his station wagon. It was dark already. Dad stood beside the old station wagon with one foot up on the running board in a position to look Phonny in the eye so that he could read his lips. A car with no lights sped around the corner heading straight for Dad. Phonny tried to tell him a car was coming but Dad failed to heed the warning in time. The car hit Dad and hospitalized him with two broken legs and many other problems.

We lived in that house for one more winter and Dad was hospitalized for a large share of it. He recovered from physical injury and was slowly recovering from his mental problems from the war.

***

I was going in to the second grade now. School was still in that little one room schoolhouse which still stands today and is used as a crafts shop on Route #3 in West Campton. The teacher would frequently inspect heads for lice. I would say anything to get that teacher to put her fingers or comb through my hair. It felt so good. However, she never did find anything. The school was heated with a large wood stove in the center of the room. The toilet was a two hole out house located back by the wood shed and the water supply was from the spring across the road. The larger and older kids would help to do some of the chores required for operating the school.

While I was in the first and second grade at that school there were boys in the eighth grade that smoked their father's pipe and should have been shaving.

One day, Sterl Batchelder, the oldest son of the Batchelder family, also from Ellsworth, was about to fill the stove with wood. Sterl was a tall strapping, back woods boy being ordered by a small black haired teacher, Mrs. Edgell. He found it hard to take orders, especially from a little grouch of a woman. Sterl went to the stove and threw the wood in and slipped in a few rifle cartridges for excitement. Well he succeeded, the entire school was on the floor. Sterl got a few days off from school and had wood and water details for a while after he was allowed to return. Sterl was the oldest son of five children. He was a real mellow person. Sometimes however, he loved to get in with other big boys and give poor Mrs. Edgell a hard time. One winter day, she found herself locked in the toilet where she had to stay until after school. She was mercilessly snow balled by the students until she had to bring in a male assistant to help discipline the students.

Fall was here again and time for that festive season of Thanksgiving. Emaline and Maud came out for a short visit to see Dad and the rest of the family. Grandpa and Mom always milked the cow and brought the milk home in a bucket. It was used for all sorts of things. Sometimes milk would be stored in a milk pan so that the cream could be skimmed off to make butter and the skimmed milk was used for cooking. Maxine, Albert and I took turns cranking an old wooden butter churn or on rare occasions we would be turning an ice cream freezer. Sometimes skimmed milk was used to make cottage cheese. The cheese cloth bag would hang to drain the cheese and then Mom would add all those spices, nuts and things to make cottage cheese. Something you would eat even if you didn't like cottage cheese.

The dinner was at Grammy's down the road and there was all you could eat: turkey with stuffing, fresh vegetables, homemade breads, cakes, pumpkin pies, apple pies and enough to make you feel like Templeton at the fair in Charlotte's Web. Dad was still in the hospital but beginning to recover from his automobile accident. Mom would pack our lunch for school and there never seemed to be any better than those packed from the Thanksgiving Day leftovers.

Grandpa had given me an old metal lunch box that I carried for years. One day while walking by the Maple Inn, Albert noticed a wire connected to a fence post with little glass insulators. Albert was a little curious about this fence so he said, "Hey Albin, bet you don't dare to touch this wire." Without any hesitation I reached out and touched my metal lunch box to it. Well when I got up from the ground, I was sure someone had hit me in the back with a big hammer. That was my first lesson on electric fences. Now Albert thought this was one heck of a good joke to play on someone. So that afternoon on the way home from school Arthur Bowles was walking home with us and with a lot of persuasion we were able to get him to urinate on this wire. He screamed and fell over and just kept rolling and swearing. It took him a long time to be able to walk the rest of the way home and he never walked home with us again.

It was not long before Mom was made aware of the electric fence caper by Arthur's Mother. We were punished and wore the welts from the whip for a few days. The physical damage would soon heal, but the part of disgrace and disappointment has never left. She would say, "You only do things to others that you would want done to you. Now you just remember that."

Someone had come to school with chicken pox and exposed everyone to the highly contagious disease. Albert and I fell victim of the disease and could not attend school, so we would fish the local brook where we were not exposing anyone. We would run up and down the brook jumping from rock to rock looking for the right hole to drop a worm bated hook. A curve in the brook created pools shaded by overhanging banks or tree roots were always a good spot to drop into. And two people fishing a brook together is always like two boats sailing on a lake at the same time. There is a race even if the other one does not know it. We would return home with our catch hanging from a forked branch. Once there, we boasted of the ones that got away.

That winter Dad came home on crutches and had to be waited on a lot. Albert, Maxine and I would bring him things: slippers, cigarettes, drinks and whatever else he ordered. We knew he could not hear us and we would talk about him or say things we did not want him to hear. However, we learned if he could see our faces while we were talking we were in serious trouble. Dad was a big man, not overweight just big and rugged. He had a big red mustache, and a loud thundering voice that could make even the bravest tremble at his threats. Not that his bark was bigger than his bite because he would follow through on his threats. He was now getting around on two crutches and did not hesitate to use them to whack someone.

Grammy and Grandpa were not getting along too well and Grandpa was staying away from home now with his relatives. Mom worked that winter and we all did what we could to save up a little. Mom agreed that I should try to save a little of the money I was making with my small odd jobs and bottle returns. Grammy and Grandpa agreed I could keep my bank at their house where from time to time I would add what change I could. This was the beginning of saving for me to break out, get an education and make the Conkey name something more than it was.

The worldly talks resumed at the supper table. The discussions on what could be done to get ahead and sometime that winter it was decided that as soon as the snow was gone and the weather allowed, we would move back into that log house in Ellsworth.

I would continue to save my pennies in my own little bank and Dad and Mom had been working on that bill at Will Avery's store.

One day I decided that I would like to purchase fishing gear at Avery's Store and decided to rob my little bank to get it. It was a hard job to get the money out and not get caught, but I succeeded. Weeks later Mom and Grammy were talking about me opening my own account at the Plymouth Bank. They counted out what I had in the bank and they suspected that there was some missing.

"Albin, do you know how much money you have in your bank?"

"Why no." I replied. Mom was sure it was a few dollars more than what they counted, so her and Grammy called me into Grammy's house one afternoon as I walked home from school. The belt was brought out and I was asked if I took any of the money out of my bank. I just could not tell the story of borrowing the money for fear of getting the belting. Grammy was more persuasive. She and Mom told me that it was okay. They were going to take me and my brothers and sisters to an agency in Plymouth where they hook you up to a machine to see if you were telling the truth.

"And Albin, if you do not tell the truth the machine will pull your arms off." Now I was some scared of what Mom might do to me with that belt, but I was sure it could not be as bad as the machine that pulled arms off. After thinking a little about the consequences, I came clean and was only reprimanded for not telling the truth. I then felt even worse because I had disappointed Mom. Of all the people in my life, Mom was not the one I wanted to disappoint. I wanted to do things to make her proud of me.

Dad had made it through the winter here in west Campton, but could not wait to get back up to the log house in Ellsworth. The day had finally come. The one he had been talking about all winter.

Mom was so concerned about leaving her mother alone there in West Campton that she convinced Dad to let her move into a little tar

During the winter Dad made many trips to the military hospitals and was granted a purple heart. He was also pensioned for being a disabled veteran. It was not a lot, but it helped him get some things including a used pick up truck.

paper camp that uncle Clarence had built in 1939 on the property in Ellsworth, which was a short walk from our log house. Friends and neighbors helped move us and our belongings, including Betsy the cow, back to our home in Ellsworth.

It was spring of 1946. Mom left early one morning and returned with my third sister, Emaline. She was the first one to be delivered in a hospital.

I was 7 years old and eager to do something exciting. Mom would always say things that I did not understand, or at least something I did not want to hear. "You know Albin, you are already great, you may have to leave some day to find that out. Happiness and wealth is inside of you. But for now, you need to help in the garden."

When we had moved back to our home, it needed a lot of work. The cellar was taken over by rats and mice. The barn was in shambles. The outhouse had fallen down and the place had grown up with weeds. Everyone worked hard that season and we even had some outside labor a couple of times. Rob Thompson from Quincy worked on the barn roof and left his initials, R.A.T., painted black and large on it, which was there for years.

The house sat on top of a knoll where it commanded a good view from all sides. To the North was Mt. Kineo, named for an indian chief who had lived and hunted there many years ago. It was a long mountain ridge at the end of a valley where the old homestead and sawmill was. To the West, a field and dirt road from Stinson Lake to West Campton, lined with large white birch trees. To the South was the old barn and open field to where Grammy now lived in a little tar papered cabin built by her son Clarence, so that she could be close to Mom. She was now their only child, Clarence had become a fatality in the war.

To the east of the house was a little stream with lots of woods leading up Downing Mountain. There was a toilet built at the edge of a small ravine there, about a hundred feet or so from the house. It was built with two holes and stocked with wiping or reading material, depending on your need at the time. Around the toilet grew lilacs, blue flag and other

Clarence, Mom's brother who was killed in the war.

flowers and lots of rhubarb. While running barefoot through the grass near there (as most of us often were) I stepped on a scythe and got a serious cut on my foot. Mom took me to the house where she cleaned the wound and disinfected it with iodine or something similar. She then taped it together and I healed with no complications, however I still have a large scar across the bottom of my foot.

The first summer a garden was planted between the house and the road. It was plowed by some friend's horses and harrowed. Children's hands, hoes and rakes removed all the grass, sod and weeds. And Mom was there showing us how to plant seeds that she had got from Avery's Store and from friends. She would say, "I wish we had…" and then she would catch herself and say, "A wish is an effort to get something without working for it." Or sometimes she'd say, "With hard work and determination wishes come true."

Ellsworth at one time was a bustling little town with many stonewalls (laid up by hand) that lined farms, covered bridges, a country store/post office, a restaurant, churches, schools, blacksmith shops and other places of business. It seemed in most all of the stories that Dad and Grandpa love to tell so frequently, there would be some reference to one of those old places of interest and they would refer to them by some unique name such as the Quick Lunch, Mead Swamp, Moss Place, Oxbow, Albert Avery Place, Ellsworth Pond and Foxglove Meadow. The names would just go on. There were many streams such as: Brown Brook, Sucker Brook, Collins Brook, Hubbard Brook and the Big Willey Brook running from Ellsworth Pond across the Willey Flat and down to Branch Brook to the Pemigewasset River. Most all streams had a logging road or trail to follow it by the remains of all these old farms, schools and places of business.

The road by our house came up from Rumney Village past Stinson Lake where there was a general store, ice house and post office owned by Bill Hayes. The lake was a clear, clean mountain lake two to three miles long fed by Sucker and Colin's brooks and drained by Stinson

Brook, which was controlled by a dam at the post office. There were cottages owned by wealthy out of state summer residents and camps, Camp Stinson for boys and Eagle Point for girls. Camp Stinson and Eagle Point were both owned by Aaron Richman. There was also Camp Wamindi, a large adult camp on the north end of the lake owned by the Lawson family.

There was one little farm at Sucker Brook Bridge at the North end of the lake. It was owned by Roscoe and Ida Dunklee. From there to our house (about a mile or so up the road) it was nothing but woods with a little flat land then down a little grade to our house. Going north on that road from our house, you would go down a steep hill and up a little grade past the old Conkey homestead and over a plank bridge at Brown Brook. Here there were cascades of water and two large waterfalls right beside the road. There was nothing but old farm sites for the next two miles or so, and there was an old, run down log house in a clearing with weeds and tall grass. Rose and Charlie Sergeant lived there with several hound dogs. Rose always yelling at the dogs with her endless chatter.

Before Dad had entered the Army, he had put us kids into the back of his Reo dump truck and we were riding by the Sergeant's home. The road was rough and dusty as we rode into view of their log house. The pack of dogs were barking and just going crazy. They were mostly hounds, some half starved with exposed ribs and scary looking teeth. The old truck, with dual wheels had a tire which had been cut by a sharp rock or something and left a large flap of rubber hang out. As the wheel turned it slapped the dusty road.

As the dogs ran along beside the truck, Bo, (Roses' favorite hound) bit that flap and was thrown under the rolling dual wheel. We heard the yip as he gave his last breath. The truck felt like we had run over a rock. Dad stopped and Rose appeared from out of nowhere. She was pissed. Her screaming was drowning out the dogs. Dad offered a hasty apology which was not accepted at first. Rose was barefoot and dressed in a patched old long dress with her long red hair hanging down and tears streaming down her freckly face. Dad reinforced his apology and told Rose that he would give the dog a burial across the street under an old apple tree. He pulled a long handled spade from the back of the truck and bent down and picked up the dead dog by one foot. He walked into the blackberry and choke cherry bushes across the street and out of sight. He was gone a spell while Rose kind of cooled off. When Dad was done he came back to the truck and talked a bit to Rose and promised to give her another hound.

The corn and vegetables were planted and we settled in. Dad still had his guns. He was as good a shot as ever and was always looking for the opportunity to prove it. One morning he was looking out our front door and he could see crows in our corn. He had an old 10 or 12 gauge shot gun loaded and in his hands in seconds, stumbling out the door onto the porch. He was still using his crutches and while muttering obscenities, he discharged the shotgun in the direction of the crows. The gun was not yet against his shoulder, it was against his crutch. The recoil from the shotgun knocked the crutch out from under his arm and he hit the floor. Mom thought he had shot himself. It didn't take her long to figure out what happened due to the loud and obscene language coming from Dad. He was forced to use crutches or a cane for a long time and he limped to favor his leg the rest of his life.

The house was one large room with a round oak stove in the center. There were kitchen cabinets and a dining table at the south end. We sat at the round table next to the stairway and ate meals that Mom prepared from whatever she could find. We ate fiddlehead and dandelion greens, chowders, stews and dumplings, poor man's bread, rhubarb pies and sauces, wild applesauce, honey from Grandpa's bees and maple syrup we made each spring.

The logs on the walls of the house were dark with oakum and plaster in the cracks. Kerosene lamps lit the main room. While we ate dinner, mice and rats ventured out to find crumbs until one evening Dad brought a revolver to dinner. He declared war on the mice and rats.

Between his unannounced random shootings and our two new house cats, the rats and mice were soon a thing of the past.

In the kitchen area there was a black cast iron sink with a sliding window over it. We never had running water or a bathroom in the house. We carried water from the spring half way to Grammy's house and the grey water ran out the back of the house onto the ground.

This summer was a change in many ways. Old friends of Dad's often came to visit: Charlie Bacon, Pete the Pollock, Jimmy Palmer, Ally Batchelder and others I did not know. Dad and they traded stories and articles.

Dad had acquired some bantam hens from Charlie Bacon, which were in a wire cage in front of the barn. One morning, he looked out the window over the sink and saw a fox on top of the cage trying to get the bantams. Dad very carefully slid the window aside and leveled a small rifle out the window hole. He discharged it and put a little hole right in that fox's head.

During that summer, I had many discussions with Mom and I begged for permission to leave home. There were so many places I could go and live with other people and work, where I could make money and attend school. She was hesitant and wanted me to stay with her. I explained that we both wanted me to get ahead and become someone, that my bank account had not grown to $20 yet and I was impatient. I wanted to get on with it.

The flowers were in full bloom and the honey bees were doing their work. While visiting Grammy on a beautiful sunny day, Grandpa invited me to follow him to learn how to line bees. He had a small wood salt codfish box mounted on a pole, a little longer than a cane. It had fine grass or flowers inside.

The top slid in a groove to close or open. He would stick the cane sharpened end into the ground near where the bees were working. He then slid open the top of the box on the cane carefully so as not to dump its contents. He then took a small bottle of a very sweet extract from his bib overalls. A very few drops were put on the grass inside the box. It was no time before the bees were in the box to collect the stuff to take back to where ever they lived.

Grandpa then took a ball of blue chalk and a pocket knife from his pocket. He scraped some chalk to make a little powder into the palm of his hand. After putting the knife and chalk ball away, he then took a small stick from a branch and mixed the dust in his palm with a little spit, to make a little paint. With a piece of straw and the paint, he would gently touch the back of a bee to identify it.

Then he took a pocket watch from another pocket. The bee loaded and flew up into the air where it would fly in the direction of its home to unload. The bee then would return for more. This was timed to tell how far the bee tree was and in what direction. With the marked bee inside the box the cover was slid shut and moved closer in the direction of the tree. After setting the cane in the new location the cover was slid open to allow the bee to repeat its trip. By timing the marked bee on every trip he could tell if the process was leading him in the right direction. We followed that bee south and up a hill carefully watching the bees load and the direction of their flight. We crossed a dirt road and through the woods where we came to a path in the woods that seemed to lead toward Stinson Lake. Finally, we could hear the loud buzz of many bees. There beside the path was a large old beech tree which was mostly dead. Up about 12 feet there was a hole where a limb had fallen many years ago. The tree was hollow and offered a perfect place for the bees to store honey and live. Grandpa then carved his name and date in the tree to claim the bees and honey, this in some way gave him ownership so that he could collect the trophy at a later date.

A day or two later I followed that trail by myself through the woods past that bee tree. I continued on to see where it would take me. After a half to three quarters of a mile hike, I came out at the north shore of Stinson Lake and the adult camp, Wamindi. The place was just bursting with exciting things like tennis courts, volleyball, archery, ball fields, swimming, boating and a large recreation hall. The first person I came to, I politely asked, "Do you know where I could find the boss?"

"Which one do you mean?" the man replied.

"The one that does all the hiring," I said.

"Well maybe you should go see Chet over at the laundry," he replied.

Chet Lawson was a tall, slim older man with a short unhappy graying wife, Vera, a son Bill in his early twenties, and a beautiful sweet talking daughter Sally, also in her early twenties. When I found Chet behind the mess hall doing laundry, he was ringing out sheets on an old ringer washer to hang up on a massive clothesline. He was a pleasant old man and eager to hear my plea for a job, but he had all kinds of excuses why I couldn't or shouldn't be off looking for a job by myself.

I was not giving up easily, everyday for a week I repeated my trek through the woods and pied my reason for wanting a job. One day he gave in. I guess he figured if I was going to show up everyday, I might as well follow him around for the company. "Ok, Albin you have a job. I'll give you $2.50 a week, new clothes and all you can eat. You come in three days a week. Your job is to empty waste cans from the cabins, pick up all the cigarette butts around the picnic area, and pick up trash whenever you see it. But first you must bring me written permission from your mother, understood?" "Yes sir! You will not be sorry Chet, I will earn my keep." I said and I was off in a dead run for home. When I told my mother you could have knocked her down with a feather. She took no time in scratching out a note to Chet giving me permission to work there and not holding him responsible for me.

I returned to work early the next day, bathed and wearing my best rags. I met Chet in his maintenance shed, which was his typical hang out and office space. I knew he was happy to see me because his conversations with me were that of a father to son. However, I could feel uneasiness in his actions. I do not believe that he had a permission slip from Vera to hire me, that part was like walking on eggshells. He showed me around the camp and then took me to the mess hall to introduce me to the chef. "Albin, this is Pinky. Pinky, this is Albin and he is going to be helping me around here for a while. I would appreciate it if you would see to his breakfast and lunch on his workdays please."

Although I was only seven I was small and thin for my age and appeared undernourished. "Wow, what a cute li'l boy, you just leave him to me, I'll put some meat on those skinny li'l bones." In all my life I had never heard, seen or known anything about a black person. When this big, ever so black, white eyed, jolly-faced woman walked up to me in her flour and food covered apron I could have dropped to the floor if I had not frozen. The breakfasts were fit for a king with choice of eggs, French toast, pancakes, ham, sausage or bacon, juices and hot beverages. She had more food in that kitchen than I had ever seen. As the days went by, Pinky turned out to be a close friend.

Rain or shine, I ran to work early every morning that I was allowed, until Labor Day when everything closed down.

It was early fall; time to pick apples, dig potatoes and collect food for winter. Meat was in short supply. We always had a cow or two and sometimes a pig, but there were many mouths to feed and sometimes we ran out.

Grandpa was collecting bees and honey from the trees he had found during the summer months. The night before he was to cut the tree, he would prepare a beehive constructed of pine boards. It looked like a box made in sections with a water proof cover. The bottom section held frames of honey cone and foundations to make more. The device was taken to the bee tree with a piece of window screen, tacks, and a ladder. With a bee smoker, fueled with moss and grass, Grandpa would climb the ladder to tack the screen over the hole while the bees were sedated by the smoke he had created with the smoker.

When all was secured, we covered our ladder, tools and equipment with leaves and brush to conceal them from anyone who might pass by. We then walked home as I listened to stories about his past experiences with bees. Early the next morning I did my chores and went with Grandpa to carry tools and supplies to cut the tree. The tree was notched to fall in a desired direction, usually to slow the fall by hitting another tree. With a cross cut saw we then fell the tree and started the process of cutting the trunk into logs or long blocks to locate where the bees were concentrated. When we cut into a spot that was hollow or occupied by bees and honey, we put on protective gloves and head gear. Grandpa got the smoker going, which caused the bees to become very mellow. We proceeded to place the new beehive close to the tree and cut small chunks from the area next to the screened hole.

When the bees and honey cone were exposed, Grandpa took tongs and carefully searched for the queen bee. Chunks of honey filled cone were put into a pan to be processed later. If there were a lot bees on the piece of cone, then the queen was likely there. This was the hard part, as it was crucial to saving the bees. When the queen was located, she was put into the bottom section of the new hive. The air was now filled with smoke drunk bees who were following their queen into the new home. It took the better part of the day to complete the transfer of the bees to the new hive. The hive and bees were left for the night and early the next morning we returned with a lantern to seal the hive and place it in a wheelbarrow to transport it home. Any part of the tree that contained honey was taken home and placed by the hive where the bees could reprocess it into their new home.

This process of collecting bees and honey would be repeated until all the trees which had been found during that season were collected. Once all of the hives were occupied they were set on a platform for the winter. They had additional sections added to them to allow for the reclaimed honey and storage for winter food. Sometimes sugar and water were supplemented to make more food for the winter. I watched Grandpa as he removed honey from the older and established hives. He was careful to leave the bees the necessary food for the winter months. All this work was to supply everyone with honey and beeswax for the next year. We rarely got a bee sting, but when we did it was treated with baking soda plaster.

Dad was back at his old tricks. He would get Albert or I or both to ride in his pickup truck at night to bring home a deer or whatever he could find to shoot. Mom could roast and stuff raccoon to taste better than turkey. We ate every animal that you might think of and I'm sure some you would not think possible.

Porcupine had a 50 cent bounty on their nose. We would bring them in for the 50 cents or if we thought they were feeding on apple tree shoots or some clean diet, we would skin them and they would be cooked to become a tasty main course in the next meal.

By the time school was to start, Dad had arranged for us to walk to Roscoe Dunklee's and meet a bus to travel to Rumney Village to go to school in a larger two room school house, grades one and two in one room and three and four in the other. I was in grade three and my teacher was Mary Russell. Her sister Ruth Russell was the teacher for grades one and two. The two old ladies were teachers for everybody's parents and for some kid's grandparents and believe me they looked it. Nevertheless, they would remain teachers for years to come. That school in later years was torn down and a new one was built in their honor. They ruled with an iron fist and I fail to remember much of school in those two years other than discipline. I met many friends that remained friends for life, however I always thought of that school as a failure in teaching much.

Hunting season was legally open now and there were other people coming into Ellsworth to try to kill the game there, of which Dad thought was his food. They parked their vehicles by trails that were notable good hunting areas, then left it to go into the woods. They often returned to find their vehicle vandalized without mercy.

That winter we cut ice on Stinson Lake and packed it in sawdust in an icehouse that we built with Dad between our barn and the path that led to Grammy's house. The hand sawing of ice, pulling it up the bank and loading it into the pickup truck was a cold, risky job around the lake. Many times the ice was pulled up the chute to the truck only to break loose and come sliding back to the lake. It was a back breaking job pulling and sliding the ice into the truck and storing it in layers of saw dust in the ice house. It was a very important job, because without ice there was no way to keep food from spoiling, never mind make ice cream. We had always bought ice from an ice man, which was expensive and unreliable. The change was a good help for Grammy as well. It was convenient, reliable and free.

Albert, Maxine and I walked with our lunch every day to meet the bus to go to school. Many mornings we walked in sub-zero weather up the hill and down the other side through the dark woods, over the Sucker Brook bridge to Roscoe Dunklee's where there was a turnaround at the head of the lake. The wind would whip up that lake and drop snow in the road that would build up to 15-foot drifts. Sometimes a dozer would be brought in to break the road. No matter what, we would walk out to meet the bus, if it didn't show up we would have to make the return trip before getting warm.

The spring finally came but it was long and muddy. Lilacs and forsythia were blossoming around the old homestead down in the valley. It was time to catch brook trout. Vehicles would get stuck trying to get through the mud. They got out by jacking their vehicle up and putting anything they could find under the wheels. There were weeks that Mom and Dad would not leave the house. Dad had a homemade grader that he dragged behind the truck whenever he drove out on the dirt road. He disconnected it at the beginning of the tar road and left it to be reconnected on the way back. This was a good attempt at maintaining the dirt road to a point that one could get out more frequently.

Charlie Bacon was a unique character. Although a friend of the family, he was crude, vulgar, dirty and all the characteristics that go with those qualities. He lived at the south end of the lake across the road from Mrs. McDonald. He was the father of Tom McDonald as a result of his occasional nighttime trip across the road. Whenever you would meet Charlie he would have to tell you one of his endless supply of jokes. I believe he remembered every one he ever heard and made up two more to go with it.

Dad would hunt nights for any animal, but was always supposedly hunting coon. He either used dogs, or Mom and us kids, to run through

Charlie Bacon, Dad's friend.

the woods to tree the coon for capture or to kill for food and fur. One early spring evening we stopped by Charlie's to see how he was doing as one of his horses had passed away and he had been attempting to dig a hole to bury it. The ground was still frozen and his effort to dig a hole was in vain. Charlie had taken another horse to drag the carcass out into his pasture. After not being able to dig the hole, he prepared to blast one. He had driven a ring of holes with a crow bar and sledge hammer. He then prepared dynamite with caps wired to a plunger. We were driving a coon at Collin's brook when we heard the large explosion. We figured pretty much what would have happened and did not go back to see. We were told later by an eye witness that it was the worst mess he had ever seen.

Charlie would come to our house to swap chickens, bring us root beer that he made, horseradish, and eggs, and to tell jokes. One day he got out of control snapping a wet towel at us kids and goofing around.

Dad was not feeling well and did not want to put up with it so he knocked him to the floor with his crutch and made him crawl out the door. In his loud, foul voice he told him not to come back until he had grown up. I believe it took more than a year before Charlie dared to venture back.

Pete the Pollock would also occasionally come to visit driving his Model A Ford. I liked to see him although he smelled like hard liquor and was a small odd-looking man with his eyes always running. One eye was white and very small, probably blind. His Polish brogue was so bad that even Rosetta Stone would not have understood him. It was impossible for us kids to understand him. However, on a visit one day he was carrying on to Dad that someone had stolen his automobile battery on the way to visit us, but actually he must have lost it driving through the mud.

At Grammy's, Clarence and a friend had built on a bedroom and were also building a woodshed and chicken coop, as well as a new outdoor toilet. She got her spring dug out and put in an old barrel with the heads removed for a well casing. She had the best home that she probably ever had.

Dad purchased an old Model A Doodle Bug to plow the garden bigger than ever. We would connect an old horse drawn single plow to the rear of the tractor and someone, Albert or me, would hold the plow handles while the tractor would pull it back and forth across the garden spot. He also got an old horse drawn mowing machine, hay rake and other farming equipment to make life a little easier. I was just looking forward to the day school was out and the camp would open again.

We cut hay on the fields near the lake and all the way up past White Mountain Apple Orchard. The old doodle bug pulled a mowing machine and a drop rake making the job so much easier than doing it all by hand. The hay was loaded onto a hay wagon and pulled home. Sometimes Albert and I would ride on the top of the load all the way back to the barn. It was loose hay and had to be pitch forked into the barn depending on the weather. It took weeks to complete the task. I loved the smell of the new mown hay. We filled the barn to the rafters with it and Albert, Sylvia, George and I often crawled through a tunnel which we made to lay near the roof where we would lay on a stormy day. It was very relaxing to hear the rain on the roof. We would share our dreams and grievances and sometimes fall asleep.

George and I were outside the door, picking up loose hay and putting it into the barn. Someone threw a pitch fork down the hole. I heard George give a loud scream of pain. At the time, I was walking away from the barn as the job of stowing the hay was done. At the sound of his scream, I turned to see him struggling to pull the fork from his thigh and screaming at the top of his lungs. Everyone jumped to the rescue and Mom came on the run. She removed the fork and determined it had entered the thigh on an angle and had not done bone damage. She rushed him into the house where she washed and disinfected the wound. She repeatedly disinfected the puncture for days until it was healed.

There were no chain saws then and we cut wood by cross cut or bucksaw. That was a real chore and spring offered a change from that job as well. In its place weeding and cultivating a garden seemed to eat up all the spare time.

Finally, in the last week of June, I ran through the woods to Camp Wamindi. There parked in the driveway was a brand new 1948 Pontiac Beach Wagon, shiny oak sides, cream-colored hood and fenders with the Pontiac Indian hood ornament. I ran down to check it out and Chet came out to greet me. He was there all alone to open the camp by July 1st and he was pleased to see me.

The buildings at the camp were mostly novelty siding on studs stained brown inside and out with shutters over screened opening or windows. A large piston pump pumped a lot of the water from the lake. Chet would make a list of all the repairs and improvements to be done in order to open on time. He might hire a little help but in most cases he did it all with only my help.

I worked longer and more days the second season. Chet took me just about everywhere with him, confiding in me all his family problems and treating me like a real friend. He bought me a blue and white striped tee shirt, shorts, trousers and sneakers to be worn only at work and to go places with him.

Pinky showed up one morning right on cue and got the kitchen ship shape and ready to serve her delicious foods. Vera, Bill and Sally showed up with Uncle Wilbur Clark, Uncle Ernie, Aunt Phyllis and a boy my age, Bobby. Everyone was a teacher somewhere and helped with the coaching and supervision of the camp. Phyllis and Vera did the office work, Sally and her friends waited on tables. Wilbur, Ernie and Bill took care of games, boating and swimming. Chet made sure everything was running smoothly. Chet and I opened and closed the camp each season; painted wharfs, boat docks, canoes and the building. We also kept the beaches and grounds clean, we did the laundry and cleaned every cottage after the campers left and made the beds up in preparation for the next camper to come. We swept and waxed the dance hall floor where I used to try to play the piano.

It seemed that Chet's only enjoyment in the camp was to have Sally kiss him as a loving daughter. He also would drive his new Beech Wagon to go pick up campers at the railroad station and tell his little jokes and things of interest on his trips every Wednesday. He loved political jokes and repeated them often. He would tell the history of everything he drove by in the car to his captive audience. "This is Stinson Lake named after an early explorer, David Stinson. He settled here and was chased by a band of Indians down by what is now known as Stinson Brook. He was killed and scalped," he would say. In addition, he would elaborate on the historical sites, the geographical aspect of the area and other things that he thought should be interesting to the campers. His stories were always in good taste in so far as there was no bedroom humor or bad language.

One story was that on a flight across the United States, President Truman and Margaret were traveling over Chicago and the president was making comments to Margaret about how he might make the people of Chicago happy. He said to Margaret, "Maybe if I were to throw out a one hundred dollar bill someone would find it and be very happy." Margaret suggested, "Well Dear if you were to throw out a lot of hundred dollar bills it would make a lot of people happy." A fellow passenger who had been listening in on their conversation loudly proclaimed, "Why don't you jump out and make the whole damn country happy."

On one occasion, Chet stopped in Plymouth at the gas station to refuel his Beech Wagon. He left me alone in the automobile and ran across the street to York's Drug Store to get something. The engine was still running and the radio was playing. I was so overwhelmed with curiosity by all the shiny knobs, dials and levers on this sophisticated machine that I just reached out and pulled the lever in the middle on the floor. There was a grating noise and the wagon lurched ahead toward Main Street. It lurched across the street jerking and finally stalling as it bumped the big concrete curb on the other side of the street. Chet had heard the commotion from the drug store and came running, yelling and looking so angry. I had known Chet for a couple of seasons now and never had an incident where I had to be reprimanded. I felt like I did when I had taken the money from my little bank at Grammy's years before. I wanted to deny any wrongdoing and pass it off as a mysterious malfunction of the car.

Chet's station wagon was his pride and he washed, waxed and buffed it quite frequently to make sure it would look good for picking up campers and traveling around on business. Sometimes he would do a good job repairing damaged oak on the wood body. He even varnished it with his boat varnish. It always looked good and he was proud of it. The impact of the Beech Wagon bumping the curb had sent me sprawling on the dash.

The sight of Chet's face was more than I could bear and I was forced to show tears of my shame. There was no use in trying that piggy bank stunt again. I was not sure that dismembering lie detector machine was not right here in Plymouth. I was very shocked when I found that Chet's main concern was for me. He was checking me out for injury and saying, "Albin, are you okay? Boy, you sure are not ready to drive yet! I guess you better go with me from now on." I was eight or so at the time but had not ridden in the front of a vehicle before. Chet then quickly moved the Beech Wagon to a less conspicuous place where he got out and inspected the car for damages. The front bumper had those two chrome bumper horns and one had been loosened by the impact on the curb. Chet, all the time mumbling so that I couldn't hear, lay down and inspected the underside of the front. After a spell, he was back in the station wagon and singing to music on the radio. I was left to live with my guilt and when that burden became too much to bear a few days later, I had to confess the real cause of the incident. I was forgiven and was still the one to go with Chet to the Railroad Station and the rest of his errands.

The Wednesday field trips were a blast. We took large picnic baskets with homemade lemonade and other drinks in Chet's Beech Wagon with Bobby, Ernie or Wilbur with a line of cars full. We explored the tramway at Cannon Mountain, the flume, the basin or Clark's Trading Post with the trained bears and the dogs that went to the South Pole. We went on these trips every week come rain or shine. We enjoyed our picnics eating a variety of delicious sandwiches and just living high for weeks.

At the camp, I was eating like a king. Pinky made ice cream and Chet put it in the large freezer out back of the kitchen. He put her mixture into a container and packed rock salt and ice around it. This was a larger machine than I was used to. It was powered by an electric motor and ran until the ice cream was nearly solid. When it was finished I got to clean the paddles. What a great job, I got to eat all of the ice cream on the paddles before washing them in the large laundry sink.

Pinky was doing her best to get some meat on "dem bones" with scalloped potatoes, roast ham, turkey, pork and every Friday we had fish. I ate foods I had never even heard of: welsh rabbit, turkey a la king, and cordon bleu, just like a king. At every meal, there was singing or gigs by talented, or not so talented guests, and even the kitchen help. The listeners would reward the entertainer by throwing coins to them on the floor. The kitchen help always kept coins on a hot grill to throw at those they felt needed retaliation.

On our next trip to the railroad station, Chet gassed up with his petro (as he called it), parked the beech wagon and took me into York's drug store. This was the next shock for a sheltered eight year old. York's was also a malt shop. To me it was a large store with little containers of drugs and merchandise from floor to ceiling. There were also a couple of booths and a long marble bar with big chrome levers and containers of condiments, coolers of ice cream and things I just had no idea what they were for. I climbed up onto a high chrome and black colored bar stool next to Chet. My legs were too short to reach the chrome pipe footrest and the seat spun around uncontrollably allowing me to dump off onto the floor. After a couple of tries, I managed to keep a grasp on that slippery marble top.

"I'll take a soda tonic," Chet said to a beautiful lady all dressed in her work uniform and running back and forth behind the counter while waiting on a group of loud teenagers. "And my man Friday here will have a...," and he turned to me for an answer while listing my choices: Coke, quinine tonic, Moxi, root beer float, malt, birch beer and the list went on. I wasn't hearing a thing. I was completely taken in by the whole place. I had observed a woman who appeared to be elderly, she was working behind another counter and fumbling with the stock on the shelves. Part of her face was missing, her face was constantly shaking and her tongue ran in and out. My mind was consumed by her. There was no list of beverages that could take my attention from her. Without pursuing it further, Chet finished the order with some carbonated drink, like tonic water. After many weird sounds from the levers we were served and I was finally able to compose myself enough to take my first gulp of what I thought was the most disgusting tasting thing in my whole life. I forced myself to try it one more time to see if all those bubbles were gone and much to my dismay they were not. In my mind, I knew that was what was wrong with the woman over behind the other counter.

I frequented this place many times with Chet and learned to order root beer floats or sundaes from then on. I became a friend of Ethel York after a while. She would speak to me in a shaky voice and continue greeting me until I felt safer around her. It seemed all of the ladies loved me and attempted to make conversation.

The mess hall and some of the buildings at the camp were built on the side hill using posts to support the lower side, thereby leaving a space under the building. In some areas, a person could stand or store items that were not being used any more. Tools, athletic equipment, etc. could be seen there while walking by the back side of the building. I was picking up papers which had blown around the mess hall one day. While walking along the back of the building, I saw an old blue bicycle covered with dust shoved up under the mess hall. After my work for the day was completed, I reported to Chet before going home. "Hi Mr. Lawson," as I would refer to him most always, "I picked up the papers that had blown around the back of the mess hall and saw an old bike stored under it. I just wondered if it was being used anymore?"

"Well Albin, when I get a chance to look at it, I'll let you know."

He then returned to folding linens and storing them on shelves in a storage closet. I returned home to do my chores. Grammy was crocheting a large beautiful table cloth for a gift to Mom for Christmas. I shared my enthusiasm of possibly getting the bike, only to hear, "Don't count your chickens before they hatch." The next morning I ran back to camp Wamindi and had breakfast there in the kitchen with Pinky, she was still trying to put weight on me and I was enjoying it. I then ran out to work with Chet on the clay tennis courts. And later we cleaned and raked the beach area. After the day was done Chet said, "Well Albin, I checked on that old bicycle and it is one that a guest left years ago. It is a larger girls bike, but you are welcome to it if you can use it." I ran out back and dragged the bike out for a closer look. It had two flat tires, a loose chain, a bell and rusted light on the handle bars. I pushed it to the maintenance shed where there was a hand pump and Chet helped pump the tires. We worked on the bike on and off for a couple of days before I could teach myself how to ride. Chet would constantly encourage me not to give up and it was not long before I was riding the bicycle on the path through the woods to Grammy's house.

Labor Day came and everyone left the camp. I was back at home with Mom and Dad and all my brothers and sisters. I told them about all my experiences and bragged of the things I had done. I was not always appreciated for my favored privileges while the rest were hard at work at home. I would reluctantly work after school, nights and weekends getting in the wood, carrying in the water, helping cut ice, shoveling snow and all of the other chores. Mom was working at the cottages on the lake for Dr. Hazard, the Frolic's and the homeport trying to "help keep the family out of the poor house," as Dad would say.

Dad, Mom, Albert and I would go to the auction at Breezy Valley as often as possible. Maxine was caring for the younger ones from the time she was 5 or 6.

We bagged every rag we could find, stripping the buttons for resale and adding a few rocks to keep the weight up. We gathered all the scrap metals we could find whether it was someone's copper line into the lake or a lead sink drain. We packed the inside of the pipe with sand and smashed it flat on the ends to hold it tight. Dad had more ideas up his sleeve than I ever want to admit. Dealers that would periodically stop by our house would buy all the metals, rags and things we collected.

Many years later I had occasion to talk to a man in a nearby city. He had been a dealer in our area years before and upon learning who I was he said, "Al you know anyone with a lick of sense knows a burlap grain bag full of rags weighs 35 pounds give or take a pound depending on the fabric. I drove 30 miles and bought those rags and rocks because I wanted to help you and your little brothers and sisters."

During that winter, we carried the water through the snow for Mom to do the wash and to fill the water barrel in the house. The snow was deep and the foot packed path was narrow. The buckets would drag in the snow slopping the water onto our legs and freezing before we could get it all done. Albert was doing the milking now and George helping with the hay.

Everyone was still taking turns in the old square galvanized washtub and arguing who was going to be next. I would protest to Mom, "There's no way I'm bathing in there after you have washed those kids dirty butts in it." I always lost. The sheet made from old flour and sugar bags was hung around the tub for privacy and I would try to just wash my lower half in that tub but I knew Mom would insist on the whole thing. "Albin, you do it all or I will for you and damn it I will check you."

The cellar was full for winter and this time everyone had collected butternuts to dry, loads of apples from the Quick Lunch, Moss Place and all the old farms that Dad knew so well. The apples were made into cider and a dozen or so barrels were lined along the wall outside the house under the kitchen window.

Dad had built a bedroom and a back porch with an entrance way and plans for a new two-holler was under way to be connected to a shed on the back bedroom so one could go without going outside.

We had a new battery operated radio now and the battles were on for who would change the station. We tried to change the station to hear the Green Hornet or Tom Mix but most always settled for WWVA and the coffee drinking Night Hawk. It was a country and western station and I loved music of all kinds so it suited me. I found myself learning the words and singing the ballads most every night. Lucky Strikes cigarettes had an add on the radio that really caught my attention. It featured a tobacco auctioneer with a good chant. I had been to an auction and was very interested in trying to do that, so I would secretly practice those fast chants every time I had a private moment.

I was doing my part at the butter churn and the other chores but I was constantly bickering with the other kids over one thing or another.

There was talk of the mountain out back being logged by the logging crew and Dad had already gotten the word. He had figured out how he could cash in on it a little.

We had picked truck loads of apples from all the old abandoned farms in Ellsworth. They were taken to Coffins Cider Mill, on the Quincy road in Rumney. They were ground and pressed to render many barrels of juice. Several of the barrels of apple cider had been lined up outside of the log house. Here Dad would add things to promote fermentation, color and taste. They then were left to ferment for weeks. When those barrels seemed all frozen, a hole was made from the bung to the core of the barrel. The part that did not freeze was then siphoned to barrels down in the cellar. Dad would add more things for color and taste and called it "apple jack."

A steady stream of customers came to sample this concoction. Hank Rogers, with his baby blue 1930 Hudson 4 door sedan, was a steady. He suffered from asthma and thought the drink was medicinal. He frequently took Maxine and other siblings for a ride in his car. He loved showing what a great car it was and I guess children were the only ones that were interested. One eyed Joshua Allen, a logger and wood chopper, drove his 1938 black business coupe into the yard once week for a quick visit and a cup of the stuff. Then there was Pete the Pollock with his old beat model A Ford. He was always drinking and came by for more. There was Jim Palmer and so many people that I never knew the names of. They all came in happy and joking, sat down at the table and visited or played cards.

"Hey George or Albert, go get a pitcher of cider." Dad would order as he would light up the old oil lamps showing the decor of the log house.

The round stove was so hot that the house door was open a crack for fresh air. WWVA on the battery operated radio furnished music for the evening and Dad sat at the big round table and visited or played cards while he served up a tall tumbler of his famous applejack. It would only be a short time before his visitors took on a whole new look. Some of them would have to be physically carried out.

One time Rose Sergeant showed up for a visit. Rose was a small, short lady, with a lot of mouth. Her constant chatter that just could not be interrupted and choice of bad language was her way of getting attention. She had a pretty good buzz on by the time she got to our house, which was over a mile walk. She burst into the kitchen from the back door loudly condemning, "Some son of a bitch drove past me and created so much dust that I could not breathe. Oh I have to get a drink to wash the taste out." She took what she thought was a cup from Mom's kitchen shelf. Rose then proceeded to pour herself a drink from the pitcher that still sat on the table. She was already so wasted she didn't notice that it was a canning funnel and the booze was going directly onto the floor. Mom took the funnel from her hand and replaced it with a blue agate ware cup. Without a break in her chatter other than to swallow the generous serving of applejack she had poured herself, Rose continued talking about her hound dogs, her husband and anything and everybody she could think of until she finally found a chair where she slept it off.

The Sergeants lived a mile or so down the road in a small one story log house and we visited often.

Rose and Charlie were trying to compete in the booze business with blackberry wine, but they had a couple of their customers become deathly ill from the copper boiler they were using.

Jimmy Palmer bought a piece of land next to Charlie and Rose where Albert and I peeled fir logs to construct him a new log home. The logs were used standing on end for side walls and all were cut under 8 feet. It made an interesting looking house. Jimmy was proud of it and maintained it well. There were old tools, window boxes, antlers and items hung on the outside to help decorate it. He worked at the Plymouth Hospital and spent a lot of time at our house drinking and playing cards.

Charlie Cutting came to protest to Dad that his logging crew was constantly drunk and that he would supply Dad with a large pile of firewood if he could help him control that problem to just weekends. Dad thought that was a good deal because the barrels were mostly empty now anyway.

Albert and I had started our new little enterprise now. As we walked to the school bus, we set traps in the ledges to catch porcupine and collect noses to turn in for bounty, this was a practice we would do for years to come. Bounties were fifty cents and that was quite a bit then.

We collected skin from their nose to present to the town selectmen as proof of the kill.

Grammy kept a flock of laying hens in a coop that her son had built before the war. It was a great building, big enough to house a couple dozen or more. She always had clean and healthy looking hens. They were Barred Rocks and Rhode Island Reds at most times. They provided large brown eggs to supply her house as well as some for sale.

Mom was also doing the same. She would set at the table and study a colorful catalog showing chicks, ducks and the like. She would order them in the early spring of most every year. And the excitement and anticipation would make everyone anxious to see the real chicks and ducklings. In a few days a shallow wood box with holes bored all around would show up at the post office. On a routine trip to the post office at Stinson Lake, Dad would pick up the box and bring it home. Mom had prepared a tub or large wood box with a homemade brooder. Most always they were kept warm by a crock jug filled with very hot water and wrapped with a rag. The box was opened to expose a dozen or more chicks or ducklings. Fuzzy little peeping bodies cuddled into a ball in the excelsior to stay warm. They were placed into their new home with special food and water in a homemade dispenser. Here they were the main attraction for everyone and put a smile on their faces. They stayed in the house for a few weeks growing like a weed until they were ready to relocate to a pen outside.

One muddy school day while walking to school, I met Roscoe Dunklee, a big beer bellied man riding a cow and as he dismounted on Sucker Brook Bridge he visited with me and proceeded to tell me how smart his cow was. I have to admit she was trained. He asked her an easy math problem and the cow would tap the answer out on the plank bridge and after a few more performances he was off up the drive toward his barn. Rosco and Ida had an old Star Motor Car. One time while walking alone in the rain, he gave me a ride to Bill Hayes General Store. The windshield wipers had not worked for years and there was a piece of clothes line rope connected to the only wiper on the drivers side and in his door window. There was another piece of rope from that wiper in the passenger door window and as we went down the road he yelled, "Pull, pull, pull," in his big thunderous voice. In between he would pull the rope in his window to operate the wipers and wipe the rain off the windshield.

Henry Sawyer was still ill and Grammy was doing her chores by herself and taking care of him. Plus she helped Mom whenever she went to clean houses for money. I started my plea to help Grammy with her chores; I'd carry the wood and water in exchange for room and board.

The log house was small and Dad built an addition on the back of the house. It was not much of a building. A flat roof room with asphalt shingle siding and a couple of windows. It was to create a little private space where Dad and Mom could sleep. And a little entry to the main log house. It was not insulated, but it was sheathed inside with a fiber board.

One evening in March, 1948, the snow was deep and there was a lot of wind. The potbellied stove was burning at full throttle to keep the temperature bearable. Albert was 13 and I was now 10. We were huddled close to the radio to hear a country music show in Wheeling West Virginia. The battery was week or reception was bad. So we were forced to get our ear as close as possible in order to hear the lyrics and enjoy the music.

Mom was complaining of pain. She had been pregnant for what seemed a long time now. She was big and thought to be carrying twins. Mom always wore a long homemade dress and a full apron with pockets when she was pregnant. Her hair would be braided and attached in a circle around the top of her head. She was cleaning up from dinner with Maxine and abruptly sent for Dad to take her to Plymouth Hospital. She threw a few things into an old suitcase. Dad had started up the old rattle trap pickup to warm it up. Soon they were on their way as we stood at the window and watched the lights slowly fade as if they were swallowed up by the blowing snow in the distance.

With Grammy a short walk away we felt secure and went on with our personal things before finally going to bed. I was praying everything was going fine and that they would return during the night with the new twins. The next morning I was up early. I removed a page of the old Sears Roebuck catalog and folded it to put in my shoe to cover a hole that had worn through the sole. Grammy was down at the log house to assure every one was on the road to meet the school bus out at Stinson Lake. There was no new twins, no Mom, and no Dad. Obviously things had not happened as fast as they had hoped. It was the morning of March 4th and there was a lot of snow. The banks on both sides of the narrow country road were higher than our heads as we walked up and over the hill and down to Stinson Lake, the way we had done so many times before. Five of us now were walking to the bus. School in Rumney would be a long day full of speculations and dreams.

On the way home the bus was on time but not very warm. It bounced along over Stinson Lake Road pot holes and frost heaves and the chatter of schoolmates did not make the trip any faster today. The trek on foot from the lake to the log house was done as fast as physically possible.

When we reached the crest of the hill we could see Dad's truck in the distance. It was parked in the yard next to the house. We were in a mad dash down the hill and up the drive. We were eager to find out what was going on.

We did not have to wait long to get answers; we could hear our new brother wailing from inside. Dad was in a bad mood yelling: "Keep the doors shut. Get some wood in here. Carry the water and do it now!" We all pitched in and made fast work of it.

Mom had a hard time delivering Jonathan. He was a large baby, the largest newborn the doctor had ever seen. Mom was trying to breast feed, but had to supplement with cow's milk and a formula which the doctor had temporarily prescribed.

Mom and I had one of our pep talks and as I sat there trying to explain what I should be doing with my life, she interrupted me. "You know Grammy would like you to move in to help her." This was a welcome surprise. Grammy was an excellent cook; she was also into teaching me all she knew. I carried her wood and water with no problems, and she did not require as much wood and water as we did at home. The house was only two rooms and I shared the bedroom with her and her friend. My bed was divided by hanging sheets like the bathing area at Mom's house. The toilet was a new two-haler south of the house about 30 yards or so. I was knitting mittens, using yarn which had been salvaged from an old discarded sweater, and needles made from heavy wire. I also made socks and other small items. Knitting and cooking was a good pastime. I could create things and talk to Grammy at the same time.

I read my bird books and got ideas to build bird houses. I used the shed next to the chicken coop to work in. If there was any scrap boards anywhere around, I would save them and cut them up to construct a one of a kind bird house. I painted them and took them to Avery's general store where he sold them for me. Will Avery was a kind person and would do anything to help us. "Hey Albin, how did you make the hole in this bird house? It looks like a woodpecker did it."

"I just drilled a lot of little holes in a circle and chiseled out the center," was my explanation. "Well, they look more natural," he said as he put them in his big front window. This was an enterprise that I did for a while and when I quit, Dad tried it for years.

Grammy was living with a retired man, who at one time worked on the railroad. Her friend took a liking to me and would tell me stories of his railroad days and show me his big Hamilton 23-jewel pocket watch. He would open the back so I could see the glitter of the moving parts inside. He made the remark that someday he might even give it to me.

We spent some evenings listening to the old battery operated radio, but it seemed to be broken down a lot, so Grammy would teach me to unravel old sweaters and knit my own socks and mittens using homemade needles. She even taught me to make Johnny cakes, pies and biscuits.

Dad managed to swap his old truck, some fresh venison and some cash for a brand new shiny 1949 Maroon International pick up. He had been bargaining and talking for months with John Bartlett, a close friend of his to get a deal on a new truck.

Now Mom and Dad were into the routine of every Friday night going to Plymouth to do their shopping. Dad and Mom would meet their friends at Harvey's Filling Station and visit for a while. It was the weekly meeting at the waterhole. They would also go see the Batchelder's and all their neighbors. They went to the Legion, the Grange and participated in town politics. They had a lot of friends now. Most always the rest of the family were left at home to care for each other.

The spring work in the garden was on again, the plowing, the planting, weeding and fixing fences for cattle and pens for pigs. Charlie Bacon was back and swapping and selling animals with Dad. I guess he must have grown up a little.

There was a law now to prevent anyone from taking brook trout under 6 inches and limiting their total catch to no more than 10. Charlie, barefoot and in his old overalls had outfitted himself with a rod and reel, a creole with bate and was fishing his way down Stinson brook. He stumbled from rock to rock as he went catching fish and stowing them in his creole hanging from his shoulder. As he worked his way

Irene and Albert.

over the large boulders, downed trees and around falls he made his way around a corner only to come face to face with Mr. Wentworth, the State Game Warden, "Oh, hi there Mr. Wentworth, I'm glad to see you. I was just wondering, If you were to catch a bunch of short trout, what would you do with them?" "Why Charlie, I would throw them back." The words were not all out of the game warden's mouth and the creole was upside down dumping every thing in it, into the rapid flowing water at his feet. Once emptied the basket still hanging from his shoulder swung up right and Charlie continued fishing as he told one of his many jokes for which he was so famous. He watched as the dead fish floated out of sight. Charlie was glowing with happiness not to have been cited for a fishing violation.

The game warden was a close friend of Dad and frequently stopped by to share his adventures. He told Dad this story about Charlie and his fishing episode. Later Dad compared it to Charlie's version and believed it to be as told by the game warden.

I would do my best to stay up at Grammy's, but Dad would send for me to help and seemed unhappy with my presence at other times. He took me hunting with him at times to carry the game. Sometimes while riding down the road with him and Albert, he could sing like no one I knew. With the truck filled with cigarette smoke he would sing those bad military cadence songs and hymns or the music from WWVA. The next minute he was like a different person. "Boy, why the hell are you so small. Must be that the best of you ran down your mother's leg. Ha ha," in his big deep, scary voice. I passed it off as a result of his war injury and did not offer an answer. The smoke would cause my eyes to run and gave me a headache. I could not wait to get home and run up to Grammy's.

I had bought a pair of White King pigeons and built them a large house on a pole, similar to a very large bird house. I closed them inside, where I fed and watered them for a week or so. When I felt confident that they would not leave, I released them. They flew high into the air and I thought I had lost them for good. After what seemed a long time

I looked out of the house to see one at the pigeon house eating. The other one was soon doing the same. They lived with us for years and helped to build a small flock which I bought and sold.

Evenings after school, I would frequently run the long path through the woods to see if Chet Lawson was up for the season yet. On the way back I picked a bouquet of lady slippers or lilly of the valley, purple violets or what might be in blossom, to give Grammy for the table.

***

Finally, the last of June came and I was back at work at the camp. There were not a lot of changes this summer other than Grammy's friend moved into a home and passed away. Grammy and I were alone in the evenings now and the news had traveled for miles.

One hot, sunny day I was picking up papers and cigarette butts around the entrance to the mess hall using a cane with a spike in the end of it. The grass was lush and green and the flowers around the brown stained building were thick and colorful. I was having a hard time getting the butts out of them where the smokers would flick them on the way into the hall. I heard a truck rumbling up the steep gravel hill from the lake and turn into the mess hall parking lot. I did not look up until I had finished my chores and by then the vehicle had disappeared around the corner of the building.

I walked around the building with my can and trash bag to empty into the barrel and saw this 1934 green pickup with a full cover over the back with rolled up canvas sides and back. From the back, a set of hanging scales was still swinging from the jostling of that rough road. The body of the truck was laden with ice and the ice was nearly completely covered with fish and fish parts, bigger than any fish that I had ever seen.

A tall thin man in a felt hat stepped out of the passenger side of the truck and although I had not seen him in years, I recognized him immediately. He was awkward and hesitant to initiate a conversation. In his tattered work clothes and wide suspenders, he stood before me for a while and just stared. Finally, in a pleading first sentence he asked,

"Do you think that Grammy would let me come and talk to her now?" However, I was quick to come back with, "Get rid of that fish smell and clean up and I'll bet you have a better chance of moving right back in than you think." I told Grammy of the incident then I walked down the path to the log house that evening and that was the end of the conversation.

I rode the bike that Chet gave me back and forth to work, did my chores and fished every stream around, sometimes with Bobby, other times with Albert and sometimes alone, always putting those little brook trout in Grammy's ice box.

I kept busy and out of the house a lot during the summer. Then one evening I came home from the camp and as I pedaled my bike up Grammy's long drive with the grass growing in the center of it, I could smell something cooking that was sending my taste buds into a frenzy. I could hear voices inside, when I opened the door, there stood Grandpa in a 'Sunday go to meeting' suit, clean hat and fit as a preacher. He had recruited Mom for backup and they had snake charmed Grammy from all angles. They had a feast to celebrate their reunion and I was out of a place to stay. I was back with Mom and Dad and all my brothers and sisters. As Mom put it, "Grandpa and Grammy needed some private time together." The rest of that season I stayed a lot at Wamindi and bunked up with Albert on the front porch of the log house.

I pedaled that old blue balloon tired bike everywhere now, even nights through the woods with a light shining form the handle bars and down the road to Ellsworth Pond four miles away, patching tires and chains, just keeping it going was a task.

At the end of the season, Chet took me to Stoneham, Massachusetts for a few days. He took me to Boston Square Garden where we attended a rodeo. After the show, we worked our way through the crowd to the ring where a cowboy was visiting with other people. He waited for a chance to be recognized and then he introduced me to Gene Autry. After a short conversation we were on our way back to New Hampshire. We stayed the night in Franklin with his sister, Mrs. Huntoon.

Grandpa and my mother.

Mrs. Huntoon was a talented artist. She could carve every bird you could think of and paint them to look as real as life. She seemed like a very nice person. She was born on the wrong side of the track. For some reason she was not well received by Vera and her family. Chet would confide in me on our trips alone because I was a good listener.

That fall, Dad was heavy into night hunting and we would take a couple of dogs to get raccoon. Dad had a wire haired terrier that was a terror and a real threat to the raccoon population. Breezy would jump from the truck and catch the coon before he could get to a tree. They would be entrenched in a fight and we would throw a blanket over the coon. We then rolled the coon up in the blanket and threw it into a cage in the back of the truck. Neither the raccoon, nor the dog, were ever seriously hurt. Later we took them home and put them in a cage to sell. The cages that lined one side of the barn would house quite a few raccoon. They were sold for the purpose of training dogs and were always in demand. Breezy was named for the Breezy Valley Auction Hall where Dad got the dog from Grigg's. He was Dad's mascot and was in that truck all the time. They rounded up raccoon for miles around the Ellsworth area.

Albert and I slept on the front porch of the old log cabin with a canvas top coverlet until late fall. After an evening of listening to a show on the radio or playing cards we would go out onto the front porch and if it got cold we would round up the dogs to stuff them under the covers for foot warmers. Sleeping on the porch during early summer nights was a challenge fighting off black flies and mosquitoes, but one advantage was being able to listen to the calls of the nocturnal forest. We could hear the voices of the wild until we were fast asleep. Sometimes they would even haunt me all night. The morning would come and the small birds and crows took over the air waves with communicating back and forth until we got up. It seemed that we became oblivious to their sound once we were making our own noise as we did our morning chores. More than once we would wake in the morning with snow on the bed. When it became unbearable, we would retreat to the inside of the house to makeshift bunk beds.

The winter was coming and it was cold every night now. We had slaughtered the hog and put the pork in large crocks of salt brine and smoked the rest of the meat to preserve it for as long as possible. The cellar was fully stocked.

Dad was into gas lamps now. This light in the evening was a little whiter and brighter. The gas fuel was not as smelly as the smokey oil from the kerosene lamps. However, most mornings there was the smell of those stinking slop jars and chamber pots that had to be cleaned. Mom was working hard washing bare pine floors with an eye burning mixture which bleached the floor white. She had a Maytag gas clothes washing machine now and in the cold weather it would sit near the back door with a long flexible exhaust pipe with a clam shaped muffler that made a distinctive pop pop noise. It reached out the door and laid on the back deck. It made a lot of noise when it was running, and could be heard nearly a mile away.

Albert and I would explore the surrounding woods and fields knowing there was no threat of getting lost so long as Mom kept doing her laundry. It was like an old setting hen calling her chicks. One time while venturing at the limit of the sound from the washing machine, the sound just quit. We yelled and walked in what we thought was the direction of home and the direction that we had last heard the noise. After walking some distance and a lot of panic, we heard the faint sound of the old washing machine coming from behind us. It was almost dark when we came into view of the log house. That was one of our many lessons on walking around in the back woods. It was not the last. We had similar experiences other times, but did not have the washing machine to help us. We learned to follow streams or climb as high as possible to look off to get our bearings.

Snow was late this year, but it came with a vengeance. It was cold for days with wind and a temperature of minus 30 degrees for days on end. It was Albert's job to keep the pot bellied stove burning. In the morning he got up early and filled the stove and stayed near it to keep warm until it was burning too hot to stay there. He wore a long sheepskin coat over his underwear to help stay warm. He was tired one morning, but he still got up and went down the stairs. He stoked and filled the stove with dry wood and leaned over the stove to get warm. He soon fell asleep and fell onto the stove getting burned. He was taken to a doctor for treatment, but suffered the pain and embarrassment for days. On a later morning, while wearing the sheep skin coat, he was working on the fire trying to burn wet wood when Dad came in to the room in a mad fit. He was cold, sparsely dressed and bare foot. In a rage he ran to Albert to hit him but decided to kick him instead. Albert turned his back to him with the leather of the long coat covering his backside. Dad had prepared to kick him with all his strength and he carried it right to the sheepskin coat. There was a large moan of pain, but it came from Dad as he broke his big toe. He hobbled back to his bedroom where Mom carried a pan of cold water to soak it.

***

Dad and Mom had befriended a tall man who had come to the house looking for help in restoring the old Saint John of the Mountain Chapel on Ellsworth Pond Road. Roger Peck Cleveland had coarse features then and stood tall. He had an English accent and spoke of things I had never heard before. Dad and Mom helped him often. Sometimes Albert and I would walk for miles with Roger. He gave me my first train ride from Campton Depot to Weirs Beach on Lake Winnipesaukee. Dad was now going to church and attending meetings in the town house next door. The town house was an old schoolhouse. The wood desks and school equipment were still intact. The few legal residents would meet to visit and conduct business to operate the town. It was an ideal place to learn the basics of town politics and listen to local news.

I was a good swimmer now and was diving for anchors to connect the wharfs and docks for the newly painted beach amenities. I hurried around helping Chet get the place in order for the administration and coaching crew to arrive and get the activities into full swing. That season would come and go at the camp while I was watching Sally and her friends. Young men from Plymouth were courting them. Young men that I liked but envied. There was Aaron and Julian Richardson from Richardson's clothing store, Ramsey Pelingell and many more.

Pinky was still doing her magic in the kitchen and had new help at times. Bruce Beers was there and was also really hot on Sally. I would go to the recreation hall a lot now learning to dance from all the young lady adults there. The square dance caller was a big pot bellied man accompanied by a band from Warren. They could play all kinds of music. I was really into those Saturday night square dances: the fiddler, the guitar, a variety of singers and other sources of music.

Sometimes there would be plays or different sources of entertainment.

Clean up the next morning by Chet and Me. As this season came to an end and I said goodbye to my friends to go back to living full time with Mom and Dad, I gave up the fine foods and life of a king to go back to eating salt pork and milk gravy, crackers and milk, fish chowder from Grandpa's fish wagon, meat from night hunting, pickled tripe fried in egg batter and things that Mom would make up for us as a family of eleven.

The family ate a lot, but often there was not enough to satisfy everyone. We just made do with what there was to eat at the time. In the summer season we foraged the woods and roadside for sugar plums, choke cherries, apples and wild berries.

Every summer Mom would collect cow bells, lard buckets and any container with a bail and load everyone, including Grammy, into the back of the truck. We would get dropped off at Prospect Mountain or some other area where blueberries were abundant. Everyone wore a cow bell to help locate each other. There was always yelling back and forth to locate best picking areas. Mom was a fast picker and buckets were being filled and dumped into large pails to carry off the mountain when the day was done. That evening Mom and Grammy cleaned and preserved all the berries to be used later in cooking. Sometimes the next morning we were off on another location to do the same thing again. This process was repeated most every year.

Grammy had a black kitten given to her which she kept to keep the rodents at bay. He was a good hunter and would bring his prey to the door to show it to Grammy quite frequently. He was a big black killing machine. Grammy was at the wood stove cooking stew and baking poor man's bread. Grandpa was telling one of his tales of years gone by.

"You know, in the early thirties while I was cooking for the CCC camps, we kept sheep for mutton to feed the loggers. A large rogue black bear was coming around the camp and breaking in to get food. Many times the workers had tried to shoot him, but he always came back, killing the sheep and poultry and breaking into the kitchen." He was distracted by Grammy's black cat that sat staring out the screened door with its tail wagging to show anger or discontent.

"Oh Margaret, your dumb cat is on the wrong side of the door again." The air was saturated with the smell that set your mouth to watering as she stirred the stew. "Well let him out," she ordered.

Grandpa got up and opened the screened door to let the cat out as he continued his story about the bear.

"We then put a couple of sticks of dynamite in a waste sheep carcass. A trip wire was set to alarm us when the bear returned. When he returned he was blown to pieces."

Grammy was humming a song as she worked and paid little attention to the story which she had heard so many times before. The black cat was back at the door with a meow to come back in. Grandpa got up to let him in and said, "Margaret, your cat has a bird to show you this morning." Grammy was a lover of birds and dropped her cooking job to check out the cat and his new catch. It was a baby bird, sparsely feathered and crying for help as it hung from the big fat cat's mouth. Grammy opened the door and the cat came in with the baby bird. She gently removed the bird from the cat and cupped it in her hand to warm it. The bird was not physically injured but was scared out of its wits.

Grammy continued to warm her new pet, she then found a shoe box which she used scrap fabric to make a cozy little nest inside. The box was placed near the stove on a shelf to keep it warm. "Albin, go dig me some mud worms. Small ones if you can." I ran out to a spot near the spring where they were abundant and easy to dig. I soon returned with a can of a dozen or more and handed it to Grammy. After breaking the worm into smaller pieces the food was offered to the little bird, which she named Robin, mainly because she believed it was one. Robin, now in his new warm home, was making an occasional peep and eagerly opened his big mouth to receive food. The worms went in and the bird fluttered its wings in thanks. Grammy cared for that bird for what seemed to be a long time. He soon grew to a full sized robin and stayed with Grammy. She fed him and cleaned-up after him for weeks. And Robin, with little encouragement, was soon flying around the house. Keeping the cat away from the bird was a problem, but Grammy did succeed.

Later after a lot of bonding, he was flying in and out of the house. He would go out for a while and return to come in. His noise at the door was the same as the loud robin call. Grammy would open the door and Robin would come in for a worm or two, always kept in stock by me. This went on all summer and in late fall he just disappeared not to be seen again until April of the next spring. Grandpa was shaving with his straight razor at the kitchen sink all lathered up when a robin was calling at the door.

"Margaret, your bird is back." She came out of the bedroom to check it out. She ran to the door all the way talking to Robin even before she saw him. She swung the door open to welcome him in as always. He was a little hesitant at first, but stayed there for that whole season coming to lunch and paying an occasional visit. He left the next fall and never did return. Grammy talked of her friend Robin and the experience she had with him for years.

***

While reading a magazine one day, I saw an ad from a card company that was soliciting for sales representatives to sell their all occasion line of cards. So I applied for the position. To my surprise I was accepted and received a salesman sample book and all the paperwork necessary to sell cards door to door. I sold cards at the camp and to everyone that I met. It did not make a lot of money, but it helped.

I had joined the Audubon Club and The Wise Book Club. I also purchased a large book on birds. I had worked up a little savings account now and was buying most all of my clothes. I had Sears Roebuck and Montgomery Ward catalogs that showed good looking clothes that I had never owned, and shoes like the ones I had always dreamed of. I would look at the pictures and discuss my choices with Grammy before filling out the order form. Sometimes I sent cash in the envelope and other times I would get a money order at the post office and send it in with the order. It was not the end to hand me downs and clothes that were salvaged from ragbags, but it gave me clothes that were respectable to go to school in.

Dad was helping Aaron Richman maintain his boys and girls camps and with the help of Albert and George they mowed the grass, painted and did odd jobs.

Mom and Maxine were trying out pork and scraps from a newly slaughtered hog. The large cast iron kettle was placed on an outside arch where it was heated by burning dry firewood. The kettle of scraps were boiled until the fat separated from the solids. The fat was ladled off into small crocks cans and make shift vessels for storage to use as lard. The pork rind was placed on a screen to drain once all of the fat was removed. Sometimes this was prepared as a snack by adding salt or spices. The next day some of the lard was reheated and mixed with soda, herbs, fragrance and sometimes pumice to make soap, which was ladled into pans to cool. The soap was cut into small cakes and stored to wash everything with.

We were going to the Christmas party at the St. John of the Mountains Church. The season was late and the foliage was falling. It was still October just before my birthday. We would drive down the road past the old homestead and the overgrown farms, most of us kids in the back of that old maroon pick up that was beginning to show wear. Everyone was in his or her best Sunday clothes.

Grammy and Grandpa Avery.

The leaves were filling the road and the truck crawled along the long dirt road in the afternoon sun. Dad with his loaded gun barrel down to the floor next to the cane and shifting lever, smoking his Lucky Strikes and squinting his eyes to look under every apple tree where we had gathered apples a few days before. He was always looking for a partridge, rabbit, raccoon or just anything that would make a dinner. It was four miles to the church and would be nearly dark by the time we arrived. The freshly shot game was under cover in the back and we left it and went into the church. It may have been real early for Christmas but Reverend Cleveland always went to Europe or some other far away place for the holidays so he celebrated here first. The church was decorated like a dream. All the wall sconces and chandeliers with candles lighting up the old plastered interior walls with old pine squeaky floors and worn down pews. The Christmas tree was tall and decorated like none I had ever seen. There were piles of presents under the tree. We helped celebrate the birth of Christ like all the children. There were nine of our clan, five Batchelders and so many people I did not know. All were so happy that we were able to attend.

The big old wood stove was crackling in the corner and fed by Alley Batchelder who was seeing to the wood supply while puffing smoke from his corn cob pipe.

There was a young man jumping up and down while pulling on the end of a large knotted rope to cause a large bell to toll in the belfry. Soon everyone was seated and Reverend Cleveland greeted everyone and talked until most everyone fell asleep. The wait to get the presents was like waiting for spring. Finally, after passing the hat and collecting a few coins that were in the bottom of our pockets, the festivities would begin.

There were boys' gifts, men's gifts, girls' gifts, women's gifts and special gifts to honor certain people. There were oranges, apples, popcorn balls and special treats for everyone. When everyone had finally gotten their gifts and treats, there were words of thanks and we would climb back into our truck and settle down to some serious night hunting on the way home.

That Thanksgiving and Christmas I spent at home with the family. Grammy and Grandpa were there. We all swapped names in a hat to exchange gifts. That way everyone got something on Christmas day.

Dad was not pleasant to be around a lot of my life. He was harsh and even mean to most everyone around. Yet he had many friends which always puzzled me. Maybe I did not see past the arrogance. I respected him and loved him as everyone should love their parents, but he only offered derogatory remarks to belittle or discourage me. Where Mom constantly encouraged and complimented me.

I was going to the auction at Breezy Valley and practicing my auctioneering when possible. On one occasion while at the Auction Giggs, the auctioneer was a little under the weather and had to quit. So my father reached his cane over to where I was sitting and gave me a whack.

"Get up there and give him a hand."

That was my first time to auctioneer for the public. I was well received with loud applause and compliments.

I stayed with Rose and Dick Hall for a spell on the Stinson Lake Road toward our school. I had my own bed and was doing farm chores for board. It was much better than at home, but Rose and Dick were always fighting. Rose had long red hair braided and wrapped around the top of her head exactly like Mom wore hers all the time. She had a temper to match that hair and poor old Dick was always getting it. He had been injured in the war and lost one testicle. She would always remind him of his shortcomings in their quarrels.

I took it for a while, but while visiting Grammy one day, Grandpa invited me to move back in. There was no hesitation on my part. I never slept anywhere else for a while. I was finally in a position to enjoy some of the better things in life. Grammy would tongue lash Grandpa once in a while, but she was content to take her frustration out on her big black cat and my black springer spaniel dog. We were finally a family. She was never fond of Dad either. She would stand at the window looking at the commanding view of Mt. Kineo and notice Dad in the foreground and say, "Look at that pot bellied bastard."

I would wonder what brought that remark out. Then she would return to her cooking up a large pot of fish chowder from the scraps from Grandpa's fish truck. She put in a lot of different things not found in conventional fish chowder. If there was not enough of one ingredient then she would supplement whatever she had in the kitchen or was in season from the nearby woodlands.

In the spring she'd say, "Albin, see if you can find me some small fiddleheads, mushrooms or anything to add to this chowder."

"Sure Grammy, I think I can get something real quick."

Across the road was a marsh that always had brakes and fiddleheads so it was easy to find a fast supply of nice young tender ones in season. And mushrooms always grew along the path which I followed to go to Camp Wamindi. I was back in a half an hour or so with a small basket filled to the brim and she would say, "Just what the doctor ordered. This will make a chowder fit for a king and should last for a couple of days."

In the early 1920's Grandpa and his brother, Lester, built a cottage near Ellsworth Pond. It was a crude built building. It had a couple of bedrooms and sleeping lofts. It was constructed from small spruce logs as studs and frame stock. The logs had been peeled and fit together for the rafters as well. The cottage was sheathed with rough sawn boards and wood shingles. It was stained brown with white painted trim. The windows were a mix of different styles and some were hinged to open similar to the one in the wood shed where Mom had killed the wild cat. The inside had been papered with a heavy decorated paper. It was adhered directly to the boards and over the spruce pole studs. The cottage was heated by a wood burning parlor stove and a kitchen range where Grammy performed her magic. The stove pipe carried the smoke to a brick chimney built on a base supported half way up the outside wall and above the roof line. Wood was stored in a nearby shed with all the tools traps and fishing gear.

All around the yard, there were bird feeders, bird houses and beehives. Large granite boulders carefully positioned with purple violets, lilly of the valley and so many other flowers encircling and reinforcing their stature.

This was a real pleasant place to be with my grandparents and I learned a lot here. Grandpa was collecting and drying herbs, harvesting honey, fishing and cutting wood during summer months. When fall came it was a whole new picture. The leaves took on a color and look of beauty that attracted tourists for miles. The frosty nights had caused all fur covered critters to build up their fur in preparation for the long cold winter. Grammy and Grandpa had many friends here and they would come to visit or help with some of the work. There was Warren Savage, a part indian local, cousin Len Mills and other trappers that stayed for the fall season. One such trapper was Carl Bennett. He would show up like clock work when the trapping season was opened. He always brought gifts and potatoes from his farm in the southern part of the state. He was a professional and serious trapper. The sale of fur was a good portion of his yearly income and he would not miss it. He went out in the early morning laden with traps and returned late in the evening carrying a knapsack filled with critters: beaver, muskrat, rabbit, fox, mink, otter, weasel, bear, deer and even skunk were all fair game. The pelts were being stretched on stretchers nailed to walls and prepared for sale. The carcasses were used as bait or buried. There were a lot of muskrat and small beaver that lived in the pond and the surrounding swamps.

Their fur was in high demand and easily sold. The hind quarters were saved to be boiled breaded and fried in bacon grease.

As much as I liked them, and some of the other animals, I was ready to change diet when trapping season was over.

Ellsworth Pond is a large body of water, a mile or so long and a half mile wide; a lake would better describe it. It was fed by one major brook and small streams and springs. The overflow was the Branch Brook, flowing out of the lower end of the pond, under the bridge over massive ledges and down the long valley on its way to join up with the Pemigewasset River in Campton. This cottage was set at the end of a

Warren Savage with my Grandfather, Chester Avery.

long inconspicuous drive and on the bluff overlooking the Branch Brook and the large granite ledges. I walked the four miles, many times, from Stinson Lake after school to Ellsworth Pond and back the next morning. Most always in the dark following the moonlight and stars shining through the trees as I ran along the dirt road.

    It was early October and the spectacular colors of fall were all around. I had returned from school to the little house of my grandmother's to find that they had gone to Ellsworth Pond. It was a Friday night and there was no school tomorrow. The days were already getting short, so if I were going to walk there, I had to hurry to beat the dark. With few provisions and homework in hand I started my nearly four mile run. I ran down the hill past the old homestead where I was born, over the old plank bridge at the falls past the creamery and then walked up the hill by the big ledges. I could hear the unique sound of Canadian Geese somewhere over head. As I walked over the hill I could look between the over hanging Oak and Beech tree limbs where I was able to get sight of a large flock flying in a V formation as though in a military maneuver air show.

They constantly talked to each other while migrating in their high altitude flight to a more comfortable climate for the winter months. It was still light when I crossed the plank bridge at Buzzel Valley Road. Walking up the hill past the old apple trees I had walked too close to a feeding partridge under a tree very near to me. His fast flight to retreat was very loud which startled me. However, I instantly knew what it was. By the time I reached the "Quick Lunch" flat it was near dusk. The sound from the fallen leaves along the roadside were causing me to believe there was someone or something shadowing or stalking me.

It was not uncommon to see raccoon, porcupine, rabbit or other animals on these long walks to and from Ellsworth Pond. As I looked down the long flat, I could see in the evening light, a large wild boar standing broad-side to me. I stopped and stared at him with my heart pounding. I most always carried a gun, but in my rush to get to Ellsworth Pond I did not get it this time. As he stood there looking, first one way then the other, I felt that he was trying to locate the scent which he may have gotten. He was ugly. His long bristly head the color of gray mud with tusks. His immense body could have weighed a thousand pounds. He slowly walked across the road and into the woods on the opposite side.

As I waited a little while listening to the leaves, I rationalized that I was down wind and it would have been hard for him to get my scent. After a spell, I was able to muster the courage to run the rest of the way to Grandpa's cottage.

It was pitch dark by now and my mind was playing tricks on me. I was seeing things in the dark that probably did not exist. I ran as fast as my body would allow over the hill past Richard Murphy's house and down the steep hill past the Aunt Road intersection in record time. I ran on past the next farm and down another steep hill past the old cemetery and into the pond road barely seeing the old school house.

When I burst into that cottage I dropped with exhaustion. I walked that journey many times after that, but always carried a gun.

In the winter the lakes were frozen and fishing was a little more of a challenge than in summer months. The ice was thick on the lakes. In order to fish we were forced to cut a hole in the ice. We used homemade chisels, axes, or anything that was available. We built wind breaks and crude bob houses from snow, ice or limbs from nearby pine trees. Later we built reusable shelters from conventional building materials like sawed lumber and sheathing. Some were quite advanced and were equipped with creative conveniences. We had different versions of a device to aid in bobbing; perhaps a spring holding a baited line would be mounted on a wall, or supported over the hole in the ice and one would jerk the line down. The spring device would then continue to bob up and down for a spell. There were also line reeling devices. Some of the houses were equipped with hammocks to rest on and the comfort of warm wood burning stoves.

One early winter day, Albert and I had gathered our fishing gear, chisels, traps and bait on a sled and pulled it to Stinson Lake. It was cold as the wind blew the loose snow across the miles of frozen ice. The power of it lashed our faces with such intensity that frost bite threatened us within minutes. We were forced to walk with our backs to the wind and cover our faces with our coat collars. Stinson was a rather large lake and good fishing was out there a long distance from the shore. When we reached an area where it had recently been fished, we decided to set up and try it for ourselves. The holes that were used were frozen over, but were not as thick as a new one would be. We hastily reopened the old holes and chiseled new ones. With freezing hands, we baited and set our traps in hopes of catching a pickerel or perch for our efforts. We piled a wall of snow blocks to make a wind break and waited for the fun to begin. It seemed that the fish population somehow had communication down there and had rung the dinner bell or something.

Albert started yelling, "There's one!" and ran off to pull it in. "Albin! All the flags are up! Get the bait and reset them!" He continued running from one to another all the while pulling the fish out onto the snow covered ice. The crows were calling back and forth while we went about our hurried business. Perhaps they were in hopes we would leave a fish in the snow when we left.

It was a short burst of good luck and we soon pulled our traps, gear and fish and loaded everything on the sled. Back home once again, we huddled around the old familiar pot-bellied stove. All in all the ice fishing was good sport and often produced a decent supply of fish carrying us through the long dark days of winter.

We often cut a lot of holes in the ice for "tip-ups" and set the traps all over the lake. The tip-ups were fashioned from a stick of wood, a corset spring, nails, a fish line, hook and sinker. There was a little red rag tied to the spring, which would fly up whenever a fish took the bait. We (sometimes on skates) would go to the hole to pull the line, remove the fish along with the bait and reset the trap. On cold days we dragged dry wood and brush from nearby woods to fuel a bonfire. That offered us an opportunity to cook fresh caught fish on a stick similar to roasting marshmallows.

***

The years rolled on with the routine of camp Wamindi in the summer, and work and chores around the house in the evenings. Fall and winter followed suit. They came and went, it seemed, over and over again. By the time I was 13 years old there was discussion of how I was to get to high school in Plymouth, or could I even go because there was no transportation. The state gave Dad a hard time. The law required everyone to attend school until they were 16 years of age, unless they had a job. Dad convinced the state to hire Harold McDonald to pick my sister Maxine and me up and drive us out past Stinson Lake and down to the Rumney railroad depot. There we would catch the train to Plymouth station and then walk the rest of the way to the high school.

Albert was 16 now and drove a 1920's Model A Ford. He had a job working for old man Hinkson, driving a twitch horse on a logging project on the Stinson Brook. He worked there long days and it cut into our time together. It was not long before he was able to get a better vehicle. That was a 1936 Plymouth coupe with a spare tire on the back. He had saved up a hundred dollars for it. He was still staying at home in the log house with the rest of the family so he was to pay board to Dad and help with chores around the house.

Mom prepared meals and laundered his clothes. When and if there was spare time he fished, hunted or trapped like the rest of us. He was going out nights and dating, this was when I was very envious. To have a car, a job, and a girlfriend was the answer to some of my prayers.

There were three factories located on the Stinson Brook in Rumney, all manufactured crutches canes and other wood items. Anderson's was doing well and they hired Albert when he was done working for Hinkson. It was a steady full-time job and he worked there for a long time. One evening Albert brought his girlfriend home to meet the family. Ethel was a small, thin blonde, very friendly and the daughter of Dad's friend. Her father (Bill Walker) and mother came to visit from time to time. Bill was a small funny talking man with a larger wife. They sat and reminisced of their earlier days and told stories to entertain each other.

Grammy was gone with her sister Gladys, who visited often now. I would cook supper with cornbread broken up in a bowl and add milk and salt cod fish. We entertained ourselves with harmonica playing and my singing or music from my old wind up phonograph. One thing I should make note of is that neither my mother, her mother, nor my sisters (other than Emaline), ever drove any means of transportation. So they were eager to go with anyone who did.

One day I made blackberry pie to take down to my brothers and sisters. On the way down the narrow path I fell in the snow. I quickly scooped the hot pie back into the pan. When I got to their house, I went in and explained what had happened. It did not make a bit of difference to them; they ate it and wanted more. I did make more treats for them from time to time and got much better at it.

That Spring I did not go back to Camp Wamindi. Dad was insistent that I should go to work for him at the other camps and mowing on the highway. He paid me one dollar an hour. I was allowed to party at Camp Wamindi, see my friend Chet from time to time and visit Bobby also. I had it perfect; higher pay, all the benefits of the camp recreations and spare time.

High School was easy. I rode the train most of the time or caught a ride home with Charlie Bishop in his 1934 rumble seat sedan. We would stop by Windsor Farm where the hens ran at large. There we got bags of eggs out of nests along the stonewall where the hens were laying each day. We would put the eggs in the car and push the car to get it started again. As soon as the car started roiling, we would scramble to jump in to start it. One day we sat right on that bag of eggs.

I made friends with many people those years. Some would come to fish or hunt with me.

Dad and Mom had tried for years to talk White Mountain Power Company to extend the electric lines from Stinson Lake to the log house, but to no avail. There always seemed to be problems with getting the right of way to set poles and run wire. However, one day out of the blue, the loud sound of gasoline powered saws could be heard cutting the trees along the road to the lake. The workers set their poles and ran wire to the end of the drive.

Mom had a friend that she had worked with a few years before. John Dole, a son of the owner of the Doles Mill in Campton, was now doing electrical work and selling radios. He came to the log house one day and ran some wires, all surface mounted on the log walls and ceiling on the inside of the house. There was a pull chain light socket and a receptacle in each room and they were powered by a small crystal fuse box in the cellar.

The power company came a few days later and finished their work, and Mom (now 32) enjoyed the conveniences of electricity in her home for the first time.

John returned a few days later to check on the job and to sell Mom a new radio. He gave a little sales talk and walked over to the old battery operated radio where he removed it from the stand and placed his new one in it's place. He continued talking up the advantages of the new radio as he connected the external antenna and tinkered around until the radio sounded great on many stations. He then proposed a deal which she found hard to refuse.

"Irene I know you folks are poorer than tame crows and cannot afford the wiring job and a new radio but I am willing to make an agreement to take payments for three months if you could do that."

Mom agreed and signed the payments plan. She said that money from doing house work for people at Stinson would go toward the unpaid balance until he was satisfied. That evening the house was lit like a Christmas tree and the music from the radio was constant, loud and was not interrupted due to lack of power.

I was staying at Grammy's and she had not been able to get power yet due to shortage of money. They talked about it, but considered it to be a bill that they could not pay at this time. Grandpa had put his name in to run for the State House of Representative a few years before and was still serving. He rode to Concord and back with Phil Willey, another member of the legislature, for years. As times were to improve, he promised to get the power installed there also.

I was required to read books and give book reports while attending my English class in my first year at Plymouth High. It was time consuming and not something I could do around home with all the distractions. I sometimes would skip around reading what I thought were the important parts so as to turn in a brief report, but my grades were not good. So I was forced to read a book picked by Mrs. Frasher, my English teacher, to write and turn in a report within two weeks. One week had already passed and I had little luck in getting much done on it at this point. So I came up with a plan. I would take my gun and go to the Mead Farm where I could sit on a deer trail and read without disturbance, and I might be able to get a deer at the same time. The

Mead Farm was an old farm reduced by age and abandonment to a cellar hole and foundations, stone walls, open field and apple trees. It was located behind Stinson Lake on an overgrown road running east off Doetown, a dirt road that ran along the back of the lake. It was what seemed to be a couple of miles from our house. I was thirteen now and knew Ellsworth better then I knew the back of my hand. I knew the leaves and which tree species they belonged to and could recognize them by their bark or some even by their smell.

All the living creatures were familiar to me and I could recognize their calls and noises. I left Grammy's house that early fall morning with my twelve gage and a pocket full of assorted cartridges, a book, pad, pencil and a roll of fresh poor-man's bread stuffed with last night's fried fish.

The sun was just coming up over the side of Downing Mountain as I walked up a path used as a short cut to Doetown Road. The leaves were mostly all fallen and the noise from walking through them was obvious to me and every living thing around me. I walked up the hill and through the opening in the stone wall that ran both sides of Doetown Road. The blue jays, crows and red squirrels were the warning system of the woodland and they were all on duty this morning. A squirrel had run across my path and scurried up a nearby maple tree to sound his alarm with a loud chatter. As I hurried along, the blue jays and crows took over the system of alerting every living creature. I walked down Doetown to the junction of Mead Farm Road and hurried along to get to the old farm site. A little way in I came to a large beaver dam which had flooded a vast area that always was referred to as Mead Swamp. The dam maintained the water level for a pond hundreds of feet wide. Alder trees and brush had grown thick in the marshy soil around the shoreline hampering the view of the large pond.

From the top of a knoll I could see over the short bushes and see the flat water beyond. The water was encircled by birch, poplar and trees beavers love to cut for food and construction. I stood on my tip toes to get a better view. There in the distance I could see a bunch of ducks feeding on the opposite shore and my eyes caught small ripples trailing a beaver swimming toward me. I started to lose my balance and broke a piece of dead tree I was leaning on as I fell to the ground. The noise was loud enough to cause the beaver to slap his tail on the water as he went into an instant dive and started a chain of events that caught me way off guard. The migrating ducks, and geese that I had not seen, hastily took to aerial retreat and continued their trip to warmer ponds.

They were not what I wanted to shoot today anyway. I was there to read the book and possibly get a deer. With this in mind, I heard the crashing of brush and splashing of water and a large snort in the dense thicket just to my left. I jumped to my feet and raised my gun in hopes of getting a shot, but the buck had enough time to make quick retreat into the dense brush before I could get off a shot.

The day was young and I had only started. I pressed on with surety after reaching the open area of the old farm land. I would get my opportunity to show my skill at bagging a deer.

It was a short walk in the fallen leaves and I reached the site where the old house had stood. It was as though the house had burned to ash or totally rotted as little remained on the stone foundation to testify to its previous existence. There was an obvious well worn trail where deer had traveled from the hillside to the apple trees and water below. After locating a good spot to settle and have commanding view of the trail and the opening below, I took the book from my back pack, found a rock on which to sit and set about to read. My gun laid on the ground beside me. I was constantly listening to the rustling of the leaves and trying to identify the cause of every sound. Noise made by squirrels scurrying around is much different than that made by larger animals walking or running.

As the time passed, I continued to read the book and take notes while lending an ear to the rustle of the leaves. The story in the book was captivating. I had been reading for hours becoming more and more consumed by the mystery unfolding on each page. The sound of the leaves seemed to blend into the story. I was not alert and did not look up to survey the land around me. The sound soon became obvious and I quickly raised my head. I had not reacted fast enough. There was a large bear running down the trail from behind me and I was sure he was going to be on top of me before I could properly pick up my gun and get off a killing shot. With no time to think and adrenaline pumping wildly through my veins I quickly grabbed the twelve gauge and pointed it in the direction of the approaching bear. I pulled the trigger. At the sound of the exploding shell the bear turned tail and ran up the hill much faster than he ran down. I looked for signs that I may have hit him. I searched for blood. I followed his trail in the leaves to no avail. So I returned to the rock, where I read as much as I could and still be able to return to Grammy's before dark. At the house I quickly did my chores, carrying water and wood. I filled oil lamps and had supper before writing my book report. Then under the light from the oil lamp I finished the report and felt good about my achievement for the day. There was no need to share my day's experiences with anyone, because aside from the book report, the day would be considered a total failure.

My drama teacher would pick me up in his car to go hunting. I had a reputation as a pretty good shot so one day he picked me up with his high power 30-06 and we drove out to the Tripoli Road. His wife wanted him to bring home a partridge. She wanted to see if they tasted as good as I had told her. When a partridge flew across the road and landed in a tree, Dave stopped quickly. "Al, you take my rifle and shoot it for my wife."

Without thinking much about the gun, I just aimed and discharged the gun with a loud explosion from inside the car. The ear ringing seemed never ending as Dave searched for pieces of the bird to take home. What a sight.

Mom, Dad and us kids were going to the theatre in Plymouth occasionally. Snow White and other shows were out. We loved to sit in the balcony where we could throw popcorn and live it up during the ad time and newsreels. We kept our tickets and tried to be winners on bank night.

Life was good. The year was 1953 and I had just turned 15 less than a month before.

Every morning I would get up, walk down the narrow path to Mom and Dad's. There I would wait for Maxine to catch a long ride with Harold McDonald to the train station. That is how we got to school. Sometimes Grammy was out even before me. Often times she helped Mom get the other kids ready for the bus.

Today was cold and gray. The mountains were bare of foliage, as I looked north over the old homestead. It was November 6th, and Mt. Kineo in the distance was blue in color contrasted to a colorless valley below. Grammy had gone on ahead to Mom's house before me.

Dad's truck was already gone. He'd left for work at Richman's Camp. My brothers and sisters were bustling around as I walked onto the back deck of the house where we usually waited for our ride to the train. The door was open to the rear bedroom and I could see Grammy sitting on the bed with Mom who was sitting in the middle of it crying. It seemed odd to me. Dad and Mom hardly ever had harsh words for each other. My mother could be physically injured or emotionally hurt and never shed a tear, but I passed it off in my mind that today they may have had a marital problem.

Harold McDonald's pale green 1950 Chevy sedan showed up like clockwork diverting my attention to the reality of leaving for school. Maxine and I got in. It was no different from any other day as we rode by Stinson Lake and down to Rumney Depot where other schoolmates were already waiting for the old passenger train to take us to the station in Plymouth. From there we walked to high school.

I was in class just before noon and the principal came to talk to me. He asked the teacher to excuse me, someone had come to see me. When I went through the door there stood Albert and Grandpa with tears in their eyes. I stopped breathing. I was trying to prepare myself for some heart wrenching news but I had no idea how bad it really was. Could it be that Dad had an accident or one of my siblings was hurt?

"What the heck is wrong Albert? Why are you here?" He just couldn't talk. He and Grandpa were both all choked up. I was determined to make myself stay calm and not allow this to upset me. What seemed to be a long time was probably a minute or so and someone finally mumbled the words, "Your Mom has passed away."

I was what I considered Mom's pet and was very close to her. I was expected to show great remorse when hearing this news. However, I managed to compose myself as if I were acting in a play. I was a young teenager who had just lost the one person I loved the most in the world. As I rode home in Albert's car with Grandpa and Maxine, I was in total shock. My brain was not connected to my body any more. I found it hard to get the strength to move my legs to get out of the car when we arrived. At the house, there were cars and people and more coming and the rest of my brothers and sisters where brought home from school. Everyone was so broken up and crying. Dad was wailing and carrying on. John was five years old and so bewildered. He had no idea what was going on or what was going to happen next. This was a tragic thing for everyone. It affected us all deeply and created a major change in my life. Later, I heard that she had died from a massive cerebral hemorrhage.

Nearly everyone I knew was at the Rumney Baptist Church where the funeral exercises went by without my mind present; I was there in body only. We went to the Pine Grove Cemetery where the burial took place.

Later when Aunt Emaline asked for me to go home with her to Michigan, everyone else agreed and I left a few days later without thinking about it very seriously or even making a thoughtful decision. I guess the decision was made for me.

The trip to Michigan was unhappy for me, as I was still not willing to deal with my mother's death. We traveled night and day until we arrived there. The trip was ever so long and boring to me. It was still dark when we arrived. We went right inside and I was shown to a room to go to bed. The next morning I awoke, the suns rays were beginning to shine through my bedroom window. It was a high ceiling and tall painted plaster walls. The floor was of narrow varnished wood boards with a round floor register beside the big full size bed that I had all to myself. There was an old oak dresser with a mirror on the back. It was beside the bed and there was an electric lamp on it. I quickly jumped out of bed and turned on that lamp for additional light. It was the first house I had ever lived in that had that luxury. Mom's and Grammy's houses were always lit by oil or gas.

Top: George, Maxine, me, Albert.
Bottom: Emmy, Art, Jonathan, Sylvia, Raymond.

I put my clothes on and opened the door to a long hall. I went to the end and down an open stairway to the dining room. My Aunt Emaline met me at the bottom of the stairs.

Aunt Emaline was always very loving and open with me. She was standing there waiting for me to come down. She had auburn red hair and was thin with a slightly freckled face. She was maybe 40 years old and the mother of two daughters who were in the kitchen eating their breakfast. She reached out and greeted me with a hug, then led me to the kitchen. The kitchen was a farm kitchen with an ambiance of the 1940's era and the aroma of bacon, eggs and toasted bread.

The kitchen table was covered with a checkered red and white cloth with an extra setting for me where I was led to sit.

"Albin, this is Wanita." Emaline made a gesture toward an 18 year old sandy blonde girl sitting on the backside of the table.

"And this is Judy." A 14 year old brunette, sitting on the other side of the table. "And this is Albin." She finished her introduction. Wanita seemed rather shy and quietly answered the introduction with a good morning greeting. Judy (in her less than feminine appearance) was in a hurry to eat, as they were getting ready to meet the bus to go to Belding High School.

Emaline explained that she was going to take me to school the first day to get me registered and see what classes were available. The first day I felt like a freak on a leash being led around for exhibition. I signed up for my classes, took a tour of the school and got a book of school rules. It was all so surreal, I was so sad about the loss of the only person on earth that understood and sincerely loved me. I went through the day in shock by all the new things introduced into my life.

I returned to my new home after school and was shown around the farm by my Uncle Jerry and everyone.

"We have 42 milking Holstein cows and a short horn bull in our dairy herd right now." Uncle Jerry commented. He went on to say how they milked the cows twice daily with surge machines and hand stripping, for a supply of "grade B" milk that was stored in milk cans and sold to Carnation Evaporated Milk Processing Company.

The farm consisted of a stone house, large red barn and out buildings located on a couple hundred acres of good level fertile land located on the shore of Woodard Lake. It was part of the old Chauncey Conkey farm that he and his wife Sarah purchased in 1850. They were Dad's great grand parents. They and Dad's grandfather, Eli, and grandmother, Amanda, lived with their two sons George and Albert S. Conkey (Dad's father) until they passed away.

Albert S. had moved to New Hampshire, while Emaline and her husband Gerald purchased the parcel across the street and down to Woodard lake. In all, four generations of the Conkeys had resided there. Unbeknownst to me, the plan was for me to carry on this tradition.

Large trees shaded the house and a high windmill was located in the yard to pump water for the house and barn. There were plenty of animals: horses (one for Judy and one for Wanita), chickens, ducks, geese, sheep and young stock from the dairy herd.

Jerry was excited to have me there and was grateful for my help with all the chores associated with running the farm as he got very little work out of the girls.

The farm equipment was basic and in very bad condition. There was also a 1933 Chevy dump truck, a 1940 Ford farm truck, a 1938 John Deere farm tractor, a 1940 Case tractor, a combine and the necessary implements to get by.

I dove into this lifestyle with great enthusiasm, as I liked to work on different things. Between school and the farm I do not believe I got six hours of sleep any night. The school was a new adventure for me as I was the new kid in town and most all the boys wanted to whip my butt for one thing or another.

I soon befriended an under class man, Frank Wolslon, and a few other guys from my neighborhood: Leo White, Joe Michaelack and Bump Dennis were close friends.

"Come on Albin, get down here for breakfast, Jerry needs help with the milking and feed the chickens while you're at it." Was a typical start in the morning. I did my chores morning and night. They seemed to intensify as the days passed by.

The bus for school stopped to pick up my cousins and me at the road side in front of the house. From then until I got back I felt like an outsider. At school, I was average. However, I was very active in industrial arts and liked Mr. Brodine, our shop instructor. I learned to build furniture, weld broken farm equipment and build everything else that was handy to the farm. I also loved to debate and participate in school politics. I studied and knew Robert's rules of order. I was not hesitant to use them at the meetings when it was to my advantage.

After school I returned home, where I shoveled manure, ground grain and did all the many chores of farm life, as well as worked on equipment or the buildings when they needed it.

Summer came and I was a full-time farmer, plowing and tilling fields for a large variety of crops. We planted early morning to late night and cut hay and alfalfa the next. The days all ran together, doing farm work most of the time.

My friend Frank would come over on horseback and I would take one of the girl's horses and we would makeup a good excuse to take off for a spell. But it was not enough to satisfy my needs for adventure. On horseback we would race across fields attempting to catch rabbits, deer or whatever we could find and chase. I was trying to get a little fun in my life, but the loss of my mother constantly haunted me. I could hear her in the back of my mind, "Albin you are already somebody and you can be great. Just make up your mind what you want to do and put your heart and soul into it. You will be rewarded."

By now I had hundreds of rabbits that were being sold at Dennis Farm Market and a wild one in with the tame was no problem for Mr. Dennis. Mr. Dennis and I got to be good friends and he sympathized with my position of all work and no play. In one of my conversations with Mr. Dennis, he invited me to ride to school with his daughter

Joanne, thereby giving me a little more time and I could get home sooner. Joanne had an early 1940 Dodge with suicide rear doors and bad breaks. One morning Joanne complained the rear door was rattling and was not closed. Without thinking I opened the door into the wind, it caught a mailbox. Big Joanne screamed, "What the Hell!" and hit the brake pedal, which did not slow us down a bit. As a result, the door folded back and smashed the mailbox. All this caused Joanne to swear up a storm. After tying the door shut with a rope and filling the leaky master cylinder with water, we were off to school again.

I was now sixteen and envious of everyone who drove. I would get to drive all the farm equipment, but was not allowed to drive anything else. I rebuilt the Ford truck engine, the tractors and some of the other equipment and built a new chicken coupe.

Jerry decided to enlarge the dairy heard to near one hundred and go with inline milkers with a refrigerated bulk tank so we could sell "grade A" milk to Sealtest for more money. I built my first and only milk house with concrete block and cement. The workload only got worse, so after some talking, Jerry agreed to give me the milk proceeds from four cows. I received a check from Sealtest every two weeks, but it was not enough to convince me to become a farm hand. I wanted to be able to drive automobiles and be in an adventure with happy people.

At the corner of Woodard Lake Road there was an auto repair garage and convenience store owned by Si. He had a half dozen beehives out back that he wanted to get rid of. So with my experience with my grandfather and his bee ventures I was eager to take them home and add it to my workload. I went to the garage one evening and blocked the entrances to all the hives to contain all the bees. The next morning I convinced Jerry to drive the flatbed Ford down to transport the bees up to the farm. Jerry helped me with the first hive while being nervous about a couple of loose bees. He soon got into the truck and rolled up the windows. I proceeded to load the rest alone. A very bulky and heavy task to do alone. On the fourth hive, while lifting it into the truck, the bottom fell out of the hive. It was a horror show. By the time I got the bees relocated, my face was swollen from stings and I could not talk or open my eyes. After a baking soda plaster on the stings the swelling went down and in a couple of days I was as good as ever. I was building up a little honey business. The honey was sold at Dennis Farm Market along with other items I would consign there.

That summer I saved what money I could after repairing farm equipment and buying my clothes with the dream of some day getting out on my own.

Jerry was always smoking cigarettes and had a cough most of the time. He kept a pan behind the cows, where he fed milk to barn cats. They would show up at every milking, scrambling for a spot at the pan. There were all colors and sizes. Once a small cat was at the pan but not looking very healthy and Jerry quickly grabbed him by the rear legs and swung him against the concrete wall instantly killing it. He then threw it into the gutter to go out with the manure. Broke my heart.

During the winter months I had more free time and would sometimes get to go ice fishing on Woodard Lake with my friends or my brother Albert, who had moved there to work at Person's Apple Orchard this season.

Albert had an old 1948 Chevy Salesman Coupe and he would drive it right out on the ice. One winter day while going out on the ice there were many other people around their holes in the ice. It was a very scary ride as we made our way over ice that seemed to be like a ride on waves of water. We made it back to shore and I thanked God it was over safely. The people that were on the lake slowly went back to fishing after their hasty retreat to high ground.

My friends and I would meet on the lake at night and during spare time to discuss our problems and disappointments in life. Leo White introduced me to his brother, Norman. Norman was a mild mannered young man with a 1940 Chevy Sedan. He would drive us around a little from time to time and was a great listener of my stories and plans and especially liked to hear me sing.

Farm life seemed hard and so unrewarding. I would sit at the table and try to discuss my intentions and desires only to be ignored or belittled. One day I leaned back on two legs of my chair and made some comment that was not taken well by Jerry. He kicked the chair out from under me and walked off.

Jerry was not a man of many words. Sometimes he and Emaline did not speak for days and the stress would drive us crazy. I could see there was no future for me on this farm. That was okay as I had no desire to become a farmer and Michigan was the last place on earth I wanted to spend the rest of my life.

I had finally decided I had enough of this unrewarding, hard, manure shoveling life and was going to make a change for myself. I had to think this out and make a plan. I always wanted to go to Alaska. I hunted, fished and trapped for fur to sell, so Alaska seemed well suited to me. Now, how to get there? The only one I knew that might help was my friend Leo's brother, Norman. The next meeting on the lake, I started to recruit Norman and his black Chevy Sedan. It did not take a lot of talking to convince Norman that we could have a great time and make a great life in Alaska.

I saved a few of those milk checks and we set a date for about a month later to go with whatever we could fit in the Chevy. I sold my rabbits, honey and other things to Mr. Dennis. He also cashed some of the milk checks. Mr. Dennis was a jolly short man who seemed to understand me more than most. I could confide in him without any fear of betrayal.

Mr. Dennis supplied me with ammunition for my gun, road maps and all kinds of provisions to make a long trip. He also bought everything I was selling to finance it.

The boys and I would meet at the lake as often as possible to make sure there was no catches in our plan. We got all the items stored in an old corn crib ready to leave. We set a time to leave one evening and preceded to load the car with everything we could and still have the space to ride and sleep. There were traps, guns, my favorite pictures of my Mom and Dad, clothes, a couple of quilts, food, maps, money and the bare necessities to get by.

The farm life seemed to be getting more unbearable. The pressure was getting to me to get out. So I met at the lake one evening and told Norman it was on for tonight. We went and loaded the car. Norman was planning to meet me later at Mr. Dennis' market. I planned to climb out my second story bedroom window with my money and my most valuable items and run the mile or so to meet up with him and leave from there and head straight north. We did not have the minds of hardened criminals or bank robbers; in fact, we were only trying to be free and happy. As far as the plan goes, it was thought out and existed in detail (or so we thought for 16 years old). And who would have looked for runaways that were not loved? If they did look for us, I would do my best at not getting caught. I would dream of little things to make it harder for them to find us. After all who in their right mind, on a frigid February night, would take off for the wilds of Alaska.

The time had come. The house was quiet and everyone but me was asleep. I pried open the window and dropped the last of my possessions and clothes to the snow below. I then lowered myself as far down the outside wall as possible before dropping to the ground. I was quickly gathering up all my belongings when out of the basement came the growling and barking of Ditto, Jerry's Dalmatian security system. I thought this was the end of everything, but I was not going down without a fight. I grabbed my things and ran that mile or so in record time. When I got to the market Norman was waiting. A short thank you to Mr. Dennis and we were on our way. For the first hour or so, we rode quietly thinking of all the things that provoked this runaway and how we would not let anyone catch us. I dreamed of different scenarios of being caught and the repercussions. Oh how embarrassing, and I'd never get to drive for the rest of my life.

Norman was quiet and drove while I read the map as we headed North over the long bridge at the Straights of Mackinac to put us on the northern peninsula of Michigan.

It was cold and snowing and the roads were bad. But now we were at last free. I was finally rejoicing, singing and telling my stories to entertain Norman. I felt so free as if I'd been granted a pardon from prison. Now I was finally able to show the world that I could make my mark and not listen to criticism. I was a normal 16 year old and was bound to make a go of it.

Norman drove until he just could not stay awake anymore. We had past Iron Mountain and many little burgs where we gassed up and finally found a spot to park and roll up in quilts to sleep. Norman laid on top of the load in the back seat and I slept in the front. We could sleep an hour or so before the cold got to us and then we had to drive on.

We were in the upper peninsula of northern Michigan now and the terrain was similar to that of New Hampshire, with the hills and trees that I was so fond of. In the dawn of early morning the hills and country road were comforting in a way. Daylight came and we enjoyed snacking on our provisions as we drove into Wisconsin. We travelled through wooded hills, snow covered farmlands, and little towns, being careful not to attract attention as some kind of tourist or worse a runaway.

It was exciting and fun even though the Chevy struggled to keep the temperature in the car above freezing. Norman and I talked of our plans to go to Alaska, get a job and buy a place where we could do something to make a lot of money and save up for a real dream home later in life.

We were driving along the northern US Border through Superior, Wisconsin, Duluth, Minnesota and attempted to cross into Canada at every place we could find.

"Say boys where are you headed?" the customs officer inquired.

"Alaska," was my reply.

"What's in the trunk and back seat?" he asked.

"Just provisions, traps, etc." I replied.

"Got any guns and ammo in there?" he countered.

"Yes Sir, we are going up to work." I said respectfully.

"Well Canada has a real labor problem right now and we cannot allow workers to cross over and take employment here." he said, shifting his belt.

"But Sir!" I pleaded, "We are on our way to Alaska."

"Not here and not today. Now you guys just turn around and get out of here." he ordered.

We drove through International Falls and up to Emerson, North Dakota. We tried to cross into Canada many times, never did we foresee this problem while making our plans.

After much effort and time I was forced to make a new plan. "Let's back track here on the map back to Wisconsin and head South for now. We could get a job, save up and try again later."

We drove in severe cold and poor driving conditions until we parked beside the road to sleep. We covered up with everything we had and went to sleep. A few hours later I woke to pitch black, it had snowed over a foot of snow. I woke Norman and said, "We gotta get out of here before we freeze. You get the car going and I'll clean off the hood and windows." Well, the roads had not been plowed and it was hard to see the sides of the road. We came down into a little town called Winter, Wisconsin and decided to keep heading south. The road was so bad, snow, hills, sharp curves and all. I have to say, that old Chevy was great. It started in the cold and would plow through a foot of snow and keep on going.

Norman was making good progress and we were a ways out of town around 5 a.m., still dark. When we drove around a corner and an oncoming car was on our side of the road. Norman went up over the snow bank and we went sideways down a long deep embankment. No way in the world to get out, in fact we believed we had lost the car for good. We were in a pickle, the oncoming car never stopped and we were over an embankment with snow over the hood and up to the windows. After rolling down the window, I crawled out into the deep snow and cold with Norman right after me. It seemed impossible to crawl up the hill in the dark and we strained our eyes looking for a way out. In the distance down the hill, I could see a light. I decided down hill was easier and faster to get help.

We waded through deep snow covered fields and bush land toward that light in the dark for a long cold time. We finally reached a farmhouse where I beat on the door. The door swung open and I was greeted by an older version of my own mother. Wholesome, typical farm lady in a dress and flower stained full apron.

"Well, good morning guys. Where on earth did you come from?"

"Up there on the highway. We had a little mishap and we are stuck real bad." I said.

This lady was so enthusiastic and such a warm and wonderful soul to be around. "Well, you come right in here, brush off that snow and set down at the table. John is in the barn finishing up chores. I'll just set a couple more places at the table and you can discuss your problems with him." As I respectfully thanked the lady while trying to keep all the snow at the door area while removing my coat and boots, Norman was being quiet, the same old Norman.

It was a true old farmhouse, warm with the wood stove all cranked up, large kitchen table, press back oak chairs where we were directed to sit. It was warm, comfortable and cozy.

The lady continued to prepare a breakfast fit for a king: hot chocolate, eggs, bacon, sausage, pancakes, you name it, she was making it.

It was not long before John came in from the barn. He washed up and joined us at the table where we were introduced and discussed our automobile problem. "Well that is no problem," remarked John. "If it is stuck too bad for a tractor to pull, I'll just have my friend hook on with his grader plow when he plows the road by there. Let's just have breakfast, then we can drive up and take a look at your situation."

We had been sipping hot chocolate and had finally thawed from the cold walk. "How do you like your eggs?" The lady asked.

"Well, eggs are not my most favorite food, but I am sure fond of these pancakes." I replied. That breakfast turned out to be probably the most memorable of my life.

After the meal, we showed John the car and he agreed. "There is no way I can get that up and out of there, but possibly my friend Robert can with the grader. I'll give him a call." We all went back to the farm to wait for the grader to show up and discuss our options.

"Where are you guys headed and what are you up to?" Asked John. So I tried to lay it out for him without creating any suspicion. "Well we are jobless and are traveling to find a place we can stay and make some money. It is hard here we know, so we're headed elsewhere." John perked up, "Oh I don't know, I have a friend who is logging and is looking for help."

"Well, I'll keep that in mind," I said

The phone rang and John answered it. "The grader is on its way over and he'll meet us up at the car." So we went up with the shovels, chains and equipment to meet the grader. Norman and I discussed the possibility of staying there for the winter to work for a spell. We agreed it would be a good idea to meet with John's friend that afternoon. The big machine came and every one was shoveling, hooking chains and preparing to pull the car back up the hill.

The grader was so big and powerful that the car plowed right back up to the road with no problem. After a while of picking up and thanking John, his wife and friends for their help we were back on the road. We continued back to town and met up with Bill the logger, who was in need of help.

Bill was a middle aged no nonsense woodsman. He looked older than his age and had a serious air about him, completely uninterested in small talk. He showed us his operation and equipment: an old Ford logging truck with a cable boom, D9 International Dozer, chain saws and hand tools. Everything was just marginal. Ready to break down or had already. Bill turned to me, "Albin do you drive dozer?" "Oh yes, I can drive a dozer, truck or anything." I exclaimed.

"But Bill, we need a place to live. We are staying in the car. We would be glad to work for you, but we need to have a place that we can sleep and stay while we do."

Bill explained how he had a lot of land and was cutting trees for railroad ties. They were skidded to the roadside and loaded onto the truck and from there to a rail site to load onto rail cars. He was behind on his delivery because he was working alone. He and his wife had a home where we could crash for a couple of nights only. Then we would have to construct a small cabin in the woods for our own housing.

The next morning we went to the lumber lot where he showed us the old red dozer and how to start and operate it. We cleared and leveled a small area to construct a cabin. Bill supplied all the lumber and other materials we needed. He also had a small wood stove, two old cot mattresses, a table and a couple of chairs. Norman and I set to work building a small cabin from the rough boards and within two days we had a one room 8' x 12' flat roof home. We covered it with tarpaper, built a bunk bed and set up the wood stove with a smoke pipe where we burned wood from just outside the door. It was not the Ritz, but it worked and it was our new home. We had an oil lantern for light and after work everyday we made our meals and tried to improve our living conditions.

Bill ran the chainsaw mostly and was doing well to stay ahead of us. I would run the dozer when we could keep the track on or get it to start, which was a problem. My primary job was being the truck driver. I would load the logs with the cable boom, a very hazardous job, then go to the train yard where I had to drive up a narrow plank ramp to off load the tie stock onto the rail car.

I had to stand on the load of logs with a rope in one hand, tongs connected to a cable in the other to connect the logs, pull the rope ever so gently to engage a wench powered by a take off on the truck transmission. I had many close calls operating this thing. Either the log was not balance properly in the tongs, the clutch would grab or slip or things were covered in ice or snow. I believed the lord was watching over me many times.

One time a log came up onto the truck so fast it caught me and knocked me off the truck causing me to drop the clutch rope releasing the log onto the truck bed. I was sure that log was going to land on me. While driving off the ramp another time, I turned too quickly and nearly lost my rear tire over the side. Norman was yelling as only the inside tire of the rear dual was on the ramp and it dropped the last foot or better with a large crash.

In our many cold hard days of work there, I do not recall any regrets. We had good luck in catching up on Bill's workload and he was grateful. When Bill had friends that came by the worksite he would brag about how he had a good crew and was finally catching up.

While cutting a dead dry tree for firewood one evening beside the cabin I saw a couple of flying squirrels float to the ground. I quickly got Norman to help me catch them, as once in the deep snow they cannot run. We took them into the cabin for our pets. It was not long before we were regretting that move. They were busy removing stuffing from my mattress on the top bunk and building themselves a nest in the rafters. They were fun at first but soon proved to be noisy and troublemaking little creatures.

We bought our groceries at a store in the town of Winter. We were very careful every time to make sure the registration plate on the car was covered by snow or mud, and we tried to attract as little attention as possible.

We would take the groceries and store them in the cabin. It was hard to keep our groceries from freezing when the fire went out. I would put the bag of potatoes in the foot of the bed to keep them from freezing, which failed to work one night. I was tired and did not get up to restock the stove and the teakettle of water froze on the stove and the potatoes had frozen in the bed with me.

Norman was not a complainer and helped with most all the work. He turned out to be the perfect partner and was easy to entertain with my stories and singing. I remember the ballad of the missing soldier was one of his favorites. He would ask me to sing it often. I never did know who wrote or recorded the song, but I had heard it when I had that wind up record player when I was younger.

> "I had been wounded in action and they had left me
> for dead, a stone for my pillow and snow for my bed.
> The enemy had found me and took me away, to
> make me a prisoner of war so they say.

But God in his mercy was with me one day, the gate was left open and I ran away.
I returned to the old home, my sweet wife to see, this home I had built for my wife and for me.
The door I swung open and there rolled a stand and upon it was a picture of her and a man.
The clothes she was wearing told me a tale, for she was wearing a new bride's veil. So I looked around and found a letter and these words I read, missing in action, she thought I was dead.
A vagabond dreamer forever I'll roam.
Because there was no one to welcome me home."

These words I have sung so many times they have stuck with me for over 60 years. I do not know why I repeated this unhappy and depressing ballad so much but I guess he liked the tune and the story it told.

We had no plumbing, lights or radio, but I was brought up without these luxuries and did not miss them at all. We had been in our new world now for a few weeks and we were getting comfortable. In fact, we were getting along so well we had a system where we would cover the plates on the car at night with snow and mud to freeze and stay away from the town as much as possible. It seemed to work well until one warm day when returning from town we were riding along and I looked behind us and saw a police car on our tail.

"Norman, we've got a damn cop on our tail and there is no way to get away. I'll bet the plates have melted clean."

Norman's reply was, "We've done nothing wrong, let's see what he wants." So he pulled over and stopped. The police officer came to the window, "Hi boys, where are you headed?" he questioned.

"Back to work at Bill's Lumber Lot."

"Where are you from?"

"Well, we've been here for a while."

"Let's see your license and registration."

Norman pulled out his wallet and supplied the documents.

The police looked them over and asked Norman to follow him back to town.

I was quick to say, "Well, if you don't need me, I'll hike back to work."

"No you come along and I will bring you back if we do not need you. This license plate has a nationwide search and pick up on it and I have to check it out." He returned to his police car and we turned around in the narrow road and drove back to town.

Once there we were led into a small police station under the town movie theater. It was a room with a lock up cage constructed with bands of steel and a swinging steel door. The police made a phone call and we were asked to wait in the cage.

The policeman was a large burly man with a gun on each hip and a wide brim hat like an actor in an old Wild West movie. We went into the cage. He slammed the door and left saying he would return shortly. I noticed that the door did not latch when he slammed it shut. So when he disappeared from site we got out of the cage and went up a back stairway to the movie hall where we took a seat and proceeded to watch the movie in progress. We were looking for a way out to get to the car and leave, but there standing in the doorway of the fire escape was that big burly policeman. We turned our attention to the movie in hopes that we were not spotted.

It was only a few minutes before I felt a large hand take a grip on my shoulder. "You guys go ahead and watch the rest of the show, then return to the cage right away. Understand?"

At the end of the movie, we returned to the cage and the policeman was at his desk on his phone again. After a while he turned to us and said, "Norman you may leave we are only to detain Albin. Thank you and good bye."

"Well, see you later Norman", I said and he was gone. Norman and I had become close friends in the past few weeks. We were like brothers, working and living together. Telling stories and sharing every aspect of our past life and the dreams of our future. And now it was the end of everything we had dreamed of. How do you just say goodbye to Norman and that future? The words did come out, but I had a lot of problems accepting this loss and my life plans.

I was in the cage for the night. The cage and the room were warm and comfortable after staying in our little camp in the woods. Morning came and the police officer came carrying me a hot breakfast. He was not the visiting type, but told me he would be back with more food later. He allowed me to use the little rest room. Then he watched as I returned to the cage where he made sure the door was locked. He left for a while, and that afternoon he returned. I asked the policeman what I was being detained for. He said, "Well, it seems that someone in Michigan had put out a nation wide pick up on you."

So I asked him, "For what?" He replied, "I don't know, but we are transferring you to the facilities at Hayward County Court this evening." It felt like my freedom had seriously come to an end.

That evening I was escorted out to a new police cruiser and helped into the back seat. The car was equipped with all sorts of gadgets that I had never seen before, not yet painted and didn't have a light on the roof, from the outside it looked just like a regular car. I sat in the back and the policeman got into the driver's seat and a young deputy jumped into the passenger seat. "I told my wife you had this big mean hardened criminal to transfer up to the county seat and I had to run along to help escort him up there. I sure hope we can have a good time tonight before we get back here." The ride was a couple of hours and I listened to their war stories and the reports of their girls and partying. It was entertaining, however I was scared of where I might be going.

It was not long and we were in Hayward and parked at this large painted masonry building. It was a cold and dark looking place like you would expect a prison to look. I was led in the front door and to an office.

"Well, hi Sheriff Bailey. This here is my prisoner that I am to transfer to your facility. His name is Albin. We do not yet know the crime he is guilty of." Brad and his deputy were off in a flash to party and have a good time.

Sheriff Bailey was a kind family man, middle aged and built like a professional fighter. "You know Albin, I hate like hell to cage you up with the freaks in here, but I have no choice. Tell me boy, what the heck did you do that there is a pick up order out for you all over the country?"

I did not want to come clean yet; maybe I could still find a way out. I could still run. I had some money left. Maybe I could get back to Winter and get my possessions and hit the road again. "Gee Sir, I have no idea, I was just working my job and minding my own business."

Sheriff Bailey could see right through me and did not waste any time listening to small talk. "Tell you what…" he said, "...come with me." and I followed him down the long hallway and into an adjoining building with professionally built cells on each side, some occupied, some empty. "You take the cell farthest from the others cause it gets a little noisy in here at night and you look like you need some sleep."

I went inside and he followed. He proceeded to sit on the cot and tell me what was going on with the other prisoners and how he could be easy on me or treat me like the rest. It was up to me.

"I'm going to ask you one more time. What the heck are you doing here Albin?" Sheriff Bailey did not look like he would just go and wait for the system to get back to him. I felt like I was loosing my freedom and was doomed to return to the farm and the hell that I had ran away from. The only thing I could do was plead for mercy.

"Sir," I stammered, "My mother died when I was 15. I was transferred from my home in NH to a dairy farm in Michigan with my aunt and uncle. I felt so unloved and unappreciated that I left. My friend and I are working in the woods near Winter and I would like to go back there." I'm sure I elaborated on it more and Sheriff Bailey was taken by my beg for mercy; however, as he explained, it was his job to hold me until my aunt and uncle came to pick me up. You see he already knew my story, he wanted to hear it from me.

"I'll tell you what kid, I'm gonna leave this door open, you can come and go in this building all you want. Stay away from the other prisoners and don't waste your time trying to escape. All the outside doors are screwed shut. I'll be back with a snack for you in a little while." And he was gone.

This was a scary place to be. I don't care if you're 16 or 60. Concrete walls with filthy graffiti, drunk and screaming inmates and the cold dungeon feeling of a prison. I sat on the cot where I had been talking to the sheriff and we had come to know each other. I had many dreams of what must be going on.

> *How was Norman doing?*
> *Will I ever get the pictures of my mother or her gun?*
> *Am I going back to Michigan tomorrow?*
> *What's going to happen in my life?*

Time seemed to drag on, where was the snack? As soon as I thought that, down the hall came Sheriff Bailey ignoring the chatter from the cells as he walked by. When he reached my cell he laid a large tray on the small table. Mashed potatoes, gravy, vegetables and a large steak, pie and all the fixings.

"I hope you didn't think I had forgotten about you, I had a lot of business to attend to. I'm sorry you have to stay here and there will be a couple of drunk women coming in soon. You eat and I'll be back later." I had not eaten anything that day and was ready to wolf the whole tray down in a matter of minutes.

Later there was a lot of commotion, screaming and profanity to no end. Sheriff Bailey was escorting two women into empty cells. He was capable of talking as rough as my father or any drunken woman. "Get your drunk ass in there and shut up before I bust your head." He slammed the big steal door behind them and was walking past the other cells with everyone calling out to the drunken ladies.

I found myself reading poems and looking at graffiti all over the cell walls until I lay on the cot to sleep. The night seemed ever so long. I got very little sleep due to the outbursts by the drunks and oh those screaming sick women. Morning did finally come and Sheriff Bailey came by to check on me and talk a spell. The drunk women were still passed out or dead because they were quiet. They were close enough, so I strained to see if they were still there.

"What's your favorite breakfast lad? My wife can make anything and the county is going to pay for it so you tell me," he said.

"Well, pancakes are pretty good," I said.

"We should hear from your aunt today. She was notified that you are here in custody and should be here to pick you up in a day or so." Sheriff Bailey was gone and in a short time he returned with a tall stack of pancakes, syrup, butter and hot cocoa. While I ate, the two women came to and were asking to be released as well as other people who had slept it off in the slammer.

"You women can get out after you take a mop and bucket and clean those cells to my satisfaction and not until, and that goes for the rest of you drunks too." Sheriff Bailey was fair but was not going to clean up after drunks or lowlife.

The day went by and no sign or word from my Aunt Emaline. Sheriff Bailey worked in his office and went out once in a while, but we got to be good friends and he treated me well.

Occasionally, he would bring in a new prisoner and once he got in a pretty good ruckus putting a prisoner into a cell. The man thought he could overpower the Sheriff but when he finally got up off the cell floor he went to the little sink and washed his face and lay down on his cot. As the door slammed, Sheriff Bailey was rather quiet about it but he told the man, "There are only a few things I like better than making love and this is one of them." Bailey always apologized to me after every incident and would have a few words with me before returning to his duties.

The next morning Sheriff Bailey came to my cell to pick up my food tray and tell me that I was to be picked up today to return to the farm in Michigan. "They're coming to take you away, now how do you feel about that Albin?" I did not know how to answer but mumbled, "Ok I guess." He was quick to come back with "Oh bullshit lad, I know you a hell of a lot better than you think I do." He left and returned at lunchtime and remarked that they would be here anytime now.

***

An hour or so later, he came and got me to go to the office where my aunt was waiting. "Oh Albin, are you okay?" Emaline was in tears and waiting to sign papers until she became engaged in a conversation with the Sheriff. Sheriff Bailey was noticeably disturbed over me leaving and soon had let it be known. "You know Ma'am, Albin and I have become good friends and I want to make sure he is going to a home where he is treated and loved like I would if he were here with me."

I was shocked to see him open up on Emaline and would have said or done anything to get out of this embarrassing situation. She talked to the Sheriff a while to convince him it was the right thing for me. I should finish high school, stay in connection with the family and every other reason she could think of to convince Sheriff Bailey that this was the right thing for me.

Uncle Jerry was out in the Packard sick as a dog. He had a farm hand (someone I'd never met) help drive up to get me.

After Emaline and the Sheriff came to an agreement I was released and we all got into the car.

It was hard to compose myself and surrender to the idea of farm life, school routine and face everyone after I had worked so hard to run away. Jerry and his helper had a small talk with me, but you could see that they were not very happy about the situation. It was obvious that once I had left, things had to change on the farm. The workload was too much for Jerry and they had to employ a farm hand to help Jerry with chores.

Jerry smoked a lot and seemed to have a serious breathing problem. He had picked up what seemed to be a very bad cold and that's what took them so long to get up here to pick me up.

We talked about how things were going to change and how much they loved and missed me.

It was some time the next day before we reached the farm. There were neighbor friends and the girls doing the farm work.

I was looked at and condemned for creating so much stress. Jerry would repeatedly comment, "You don't know what the hell you caused your aunt Emaline. She was worried sick about you all the time. I hope this does not happen again." He seemed to go on and on. While having dinner, I was asked the questions, "What provoked you to do this? Where did you guys go? Where is Norman?" And on and on and on.

After a night sleep, I was called to breakfast and Emaline informed me I was to go with her to talk to the principal of Belding High to continue my classes there. It was not hard to convince the principal to allow me to go back to my classes and make up the work from my nearly 3-month absence.

Emaline was nice to me and said, "You know I love you and only want to do what is good for you. Things will be different. Joe the new farm hand will help Jerry with the farm work. You can discuss any of your problems with me. We will work our way through this." She was definitely more loving and attentive than before. In the evening she would sit with me on the sofa and talk, hug and kiss me. She showed me more affection than I had ever had.

She was very upset when she learned that Mr. Dennis had cashed my checks and aided in my runaway. She boycotted his market for some time to retaliate. Wanita and Judy acted more friendly to me as though there was a plan and they were to make me feel welcome so that I would want to stay.

The hired hand, Joe, was sleeping in the basement with the Dalmatian, Ditto. He was rather quiet and looked for his companion in a bottle of booze. He and Jerry were not very close and Jerry seemed to have trouble having him do the work he expected of him.

I soon fell into the routine and was back doing farm work and repairing farm equipment. I finished my junior year at school with flying colors. In fact, I had enough credits to graduate but the state required four years. So, in my senior year I could take Co-op training that enabled me to go to school only half days, giving me more time to work on the farm and have those talks with Emaline.

She was being very close and I believed she was either wanting to be intimate with me or she was legitimately fond of me. Although, sometimes she would become frustrated and say things like I know you are trying to take advantage of my daughters. Well I never did respond to these allegations, as one would have to know that Judy, now 15, was entertaining boys whenever she could, mostly in the evenings at the lake. Wanita, now 18, was a little less than right as Emaline would say, "She suffered from lack of oxygen during childbirth." It's not that I did not have the same sexual desires as most 16 year olds, but I was not interested in experimenting with my own family.

***

That school year ended and I worked on the farm with Jerry and his bad attitude, doing what I could to get by. I worked some with my brother at the orchard bagging apples. Once again, trying to save money. I sold honey and saved every penny I could. I met with Frank and Leo, but never did hear what happened to Norman. We had some fun times together and would hitchhike to school and back together sometimes, as it was my only way around. I still had a curfew and was not allowed to drive or go out at night.

In the year after my mother had passed away, my brother Albert, who had been working at a crutch factory on Stinson Brook was laid off. He was unable to find a job, so he, his wife Ethal and their little son Albert Albin moved to Michigan where he got a job working at Persons apple orchard. He was doing maintenance work and pruning as well as packing.

We were close and he named his first born after me. I would stop by once in a while or I would walk to his little trailer where he lived next to the orchard. We talked of old times of the past when Mom was alive, my failed trip to Alaska and how someday I would succeed in life without being a farmhand.

Albert tried to console me and would engage me in conversation about my future. He would ask me, "So what would you like to do with your life?"

"I guess I never gave it much thought. I only know what I don't want to do." I replied.

Since I was a child I had wanted to do something to make my mother and everyone else proud of me, but I never seemed to really be able to decide who or what I wanted to be. In Michigan, I found myself in the barn many times wishing I was back with my family in Ellsworth.

I was living in hell on my uncle's farm. Daily, I shoveled manure from the gutters and wheeled it out the back door where it was dumped in a large pile. It was a job that I deplored. Cows would come into their stanchion where they were milked after grazing on green clover or alfalfa. It made their manure so loose that if a cow were to sneeze or cough it would discharge a large mess onto anything that was in line of it. The walls behind the cows were literally painted with stuff. More than once I was in the line of fire and covered with a very bad odor producing mess. I would have to remove my outer clothes and go inside the house to bathe. It was humiliating to say the least and made me dislike the farm just that much more.

I was very depressed and missed my friends in New Hampshire. I felt that I had failed a well planned run away attempt and was not going to get out of this horrible life alive. I even considered taking my own life. If it had not been for Albert and his encouraging visits, I very well may have.

The summer soon passed and we were back in Belding High School. Senior year now and only going to school half days and dreaming of the end of this lifestyle. Although, there were days on the farm that were more exciting. I had rescued a couple of little screech owls that I kept in the basement with Ditto and Joe. The first night the owls screamed and Joe did not know they were there; it scared him out of his wits.

A little while later, Uncle Jerry and Joe had differences on how the farm should be run. So in the height of anger Joe parted company by taking his few possessions and walking down the road.

Later, I heard that Maxine had graduated in Plymouth, NH. I talked about going on to college and was soon discouraged from that idea by remarks from Jerry.

I finished my senior year and graduated with cap and gown. I was so happy to think that I had been the first in my family of nine children to do this.

"What a stupid idea. We haven't got that kind of money and you can do just as good without it."

My father and his wife, Flora, came to my graduation, they brought my sister Sylvia and the watch that Henry Sawyer had promised as a graduation gift. I was speechless and so grateful they would come, My father was the last person I expected to see there. They talked to Jerry and painted a picture of New Hampshire that he just had to see.

Ace, Jerry's brother, lived in northern New Jersey and had been in contact with him. He had offered an interesting proposal to Jerry and now he was giving it some serious thought. He had not seen Ace in a few years as Ace was in the Navy. Ace was to show him a great time in New York if he could pay him a visit. After planning and a lot of intense discussions it was decided that we would go to New Hampshire and stop in New Jersey to see Ace on the way.

Finally, there was hope of getting off the farm and back to NH where I might get the opportunity to go on to college.

Jerry managed to employ someone to help tend the farm and on the 4th of July we left for NH in the old Packard. Jerry was fed up with farm life and was entertaining the idea of going East to live for a while. I was talking to little Emmy about my plan of never returning to the farm and inquired what her intentions were. I later made a two dollar bet with her that she would return.

The trip was long. Everyone was speculating what the visit with Ace would be like and there was talk of what they were going to do when they reached New Hampshire. Emaline wanted to visit the old homestead where she was born and Jerry was into seeing what he might do to make a living if he was to sell the farm and move there. The old Packard gave a comfortable ride and had no mechanical problems.

We traveled down through Ohio and Pennsylvania to New Jersey and met up with Ace. We toured a few of his favorite places like Coney Island, the Empire State Building, the Statue of Liberty and a zoo. Ace drove his new 1954 Oldsmobile from one attraction as though he was competing with Mario Andretti, making U-turns in traffic and speeding around the busy streets. He was making it a real challenge for Jerry to follow him. A couple of days of this and Jerry was ready to let his brother Ace go back to the Navy base and continue our trip to New Hampshire.

When we got to NH we rode down that old dirt road to the home where my Mom had passed away. The old memories were coming back to me as it would anyone when returning home after being away for a couple of years, especially when you are young and remember small details.

Cresting the hill I could see the valley below, but a lot of things were different. The log home was missing and not to be seen anywhere. Another house was moved into the picture. It was located near the road and where the drive used to start. The knoll where the log house used to command it's great view was completely removed. The complete site was flatter than piss on a platter and was not recognizable to me. I later learned that Maxine had married Clarence Poitras and lived in the log home where she had her firstborn. Dad had a house moved in from Stinson Lake and had it located near the road where he and his new bride lived with my siblings. After a few months the log home caught on fire and was completely burned.

***

Now George was working at Camp Wamindi. Raymond was staying with Grandpa and Grammy. Art was still at the Avery Farm in West Campton. Little Emmy had come to the farm in Michigan to spend a season. John and Sylvia stayed with Dad and Flora.

Sylvia was not overweight, but a tall, larger framed girl caused by hard work and exercise. She was always smiling. She looked like Mom, but had the disposition of Dad. She would confront any situation in school and was suspended for getting physical with a lesbian teacher for trying to approach her with other than academic reasons.

While here in New Hampshire, Jerry, Dad and Emmy toured a lot and checked out the NH attractions. They finally set a date for our return to Michigan. Little did they know that I had no intention of going with them.

Sylvia and I had a plan in order. We were going to be gone when the wagon was ready to depart. The day before we were supposed to leave Sylvia took me to an old CCC camp at 3 Ponds. It was about a four mile hike, some on a logging trail and some bushwhacking. We planned to stay out there a couple of days until everyone was gone. It was perfect, no confrontation, no tears, no embarrassment or anything.

It was a great cabin. I only wish I could have had it (or one like it) in Wisconsin. It was constructed of logs back in the time when the CCC camps were in operation. The logs were laid on the ground with no foundation. The corners were notched to allow the logs to lay closer together. It consisted of one window, a loft, bunk beds and a large wood stove. As good if not better than I had lived in before.

We stowed away what little food and things we brought into the cabin. There was an area next to the pond with an old shovel and lots of black moist soil where people always dug for earthworms and grubs. It was an easy place for us to get our bait. We tried our luck at fishing in the pond only a few feet away from the cabin. There was a raft right next to the shore and we checked to see how well it floated before climbing on and pushing off shore to get out on the pond where we could fish. Trout fishing was my thing and it was not long before I was able to catch all the fish we could eat for a couple of meals. We poled back to shore and I cleaned the trout on a nearby rock where it was easy to wash up. That evening we had a fire in the stove and cooked a can of beans with our catch of the day.

We stayed at 3 Ponds for a couple of days reminiscing and telling each other stories. We ate what few provisions we had brought along and what we found in the cupboard in the cabin. Most people who came here to fish or hike always left canned foods in the cupboards: beans, spam, canned fruit, etc. We caught a lot of trout and had a good time visiting. Sylvia was a real outdoor type and could have probably stayed there the rest of her life with just a few essentials. Carrying water from the pond, gathering dry wood for the fire, catching fish and using the outdoor privy. On the third day we decided to get up and walk home.

We walked across Fox Glove Meadow to the Donkey Hill cut off and down the Keneo trail, all part of the old CCC camp project. It was a longer walk but along a much better fishing region. We carried a creel and bate cans full of our fresh dug bait. We found good cold damp moss for stowing our fish to keep it fresh on the way home.

The walk was great and we were able to find our way by blazed trees through the thick forest and swamps by big beaver dams where we fished and were very lucky. We finally reached a big metal steam engine and boiler and we knew we were on the right trail. The old engine was used by the lumbermen in the CCC camp to haul logs over the hill to go down the Mt. Keneo trail. From that point on, it was all down hill by the Big Falls and down Brown Brook, crossing old washed out bridges and some real good fishing. We had such a blast we were in no hurry to get back to Dad's house, for we had no idea what was going on there. We had our creoles full of cleaned trout packed in moss, not a speck of room for more.

When we got down to the last fall, which we always referred to as Conkey Falls we were right next door to the house I was born in and a short walk to Dad's house. I could not resist trying the big hole at the bottom of the falls, it was deep, dark and where we had fished and swam so many times before. We baited up our poles and threw the worm into the falling water and let it flow with the stream down into the darkness of the deep. With a powerful jerk my pole was about to break as it bent toward the water. After a good fight, I was able to drag the biggest brookie I ever saw to the edge. I reached down to grab a gill and he managed to get one more lunge for life that broke my hook and he was gone.

Sylvia stood there and laughed as she was landing a good sized one herself. We managed to put a few on a stick and were on our way up the dirt road past the old Conkey Farm and up the hill to Dad's house.

The place was quiet, no one around. We were putting the fish in the refrigerator when Dad, Flora and little Emmy drove in. It was dark now and Flora and Sylvia got supper while Dad and I sat and talked. Emaline and Gerald had left that morning for Michigan. Jerry had told Dad the first day that he had suspected that I was going to disappear so it was no surprise to them when I did not show up to return to Michigan.

I was feeling good and was finally able to rest and think for myself. No more heavy farm work. I could get my license and a car to drive, and finally be normal.

Dad told me that Joe Yeaton had passed away and the land behind Grammy's house and up Downing Mountain where Joe had logged many years ago may be for sale. I talked to him about the possibility of buying it and logging it again. He was rather passive about the idea, but it sure sounded good to me. A chance to get a place of my own. Maybe I could buy it on time and build my own little house there. It was a large track of land around 140 acres with a lot of road frontage around the back of Stinson Lake and not far from Camp Wamindi where I had worked before my mother died.

I was reading the Plymouth Record and noticed an ad for a 1938 Chevrolet Sedan for $50. It was in Campton Village about seven miles away. I was very interested in it. Dad agreed to take me over to check it out. We found it right away. The owner was eager to sell it to get it out of his yard. After checking it out and running it around, I agreed to give him $35 as that was all I had with me. He agreed, and I drove the car away. Dad went home and I followed up the West Campton Road and right up to Dad's house.

Now I had to go get a license and register the car, which would be easy. I went to the town clerk, Ida Clark, where she did all the paperwork and for a few bucks it was done. I only had to wait for the plates and license to come from Concord.

I talked Dad into taking me to meet with Joe Yeaton's widow to discuss the possibility of getting the land. One day he took me to her large white farmhouse in West Plymouth. I realized, I knew the family from before my mother had died. I went to school with her son, my friend Dean Yeaton. She was very nice and invited me in after my knock on her door. Dad followed to listen to our conversation.

She agreed that the land was for sale. It seems that her husband Joe had acquired lots of land for his lumber business and she was burdened with a lot of property tax and was in need of getting rid of some of it. I offered her $600 cash upon presentation of a warranty deed, but I would have to be able to cut some pulpwood off of it prior to closing to be able to raise the money. I was shocked that she was so easy to make a deal with. I gave her a few bucks and signed a paper she drew up and left.

The next day I was cutting pulp and piling it along the road. George was 14 and rugged. We, together with an old chain saw, were cutting and piling wood 4' high as far as the eye could see along the road. Ted Toby was buying for the paper mill and would come by every week to scale and pay $20 a cord for what we had cut. It was not long before I had my money for Mrs. Yeaton and we consummated our real estate transaction. She thanked me and said, "I hope it turns into a good venture for you."

George and I were cutting pulp and getting it down the mountain any way we could. We carried it on our shoulders or dragged it every way possible to pile as much, and as fast as we could. I was bound to raise enough money to build a house and get a horse.

I managed to get an old building from Camp Eagle Point that was being taken down less than a mile away. We dismantled it in pieces and moved it to my lot near the old cellar hole where the original house had stood many years before.

I bumped into Charlie Bishop, an old schoolmate of mine, one day in Plymouth. He said his father, Horace, had an old white mare he was looking to get rid of. The next day I went up to West Rumney to take a look. I had met Horace years before and he and his family were good friends of mine. I found him in the barn where he was cleaning the horse stall. He told me that the horse was old, but could work.

He had a loft of loose hay and a good complete work harness with whiffle tree, chains and supplies that he would be glad to sell.

We talked a while and I ended up paying him $75 cash for everything. I went back to Dad's house and told him about the deal. It was about noon then and Dad agreed to take me over to get the horse. We had no trailer or truck to load the horse onto. I figured now I was in business, I could cut more and faster with a horse. I could not wait to get it up on the job. The only way to do it was walk. The complete trip was about seven miles. I led Dolly for hours admiring the countryside, as we walked by houses, churches, schools, post offices and country stores. Up the long crooked road that followed Stinson Brook and the full length of the lake, where we stopped for a drink. I don't know about Dolly, but I was glad when we got to the horse barn where I had already provided a feedbag with oats and some hay in a manger.

I begged the use of my Dad's International truck. One of those he had bargained for from John Bartlett a couple of years before. It was red with a homemade flat rack that Dad had built. He said the truck was too good to be loaning to a 17 year old but he was going to trust me this time. The next day George and I connected an old utility trailer to the back of the truck and we went to haul hay up to the barn where it was stowed under a lean to. We loaded the truck and trailer with hay and were heading up the pothole black top road when we heard a loud "clank" noise. I pulled to a stop and ran around the load to see what was going on. There was no trailer to be seen anywhere. We ran down the road searching. Then George noticed a little hay beside the road. After looking down over the steep bank you could see the trailer upside down lying on a pile of hay covered by bushes.

We managed to retrieve the trailer with long ropes and chains, but the hay was lost. George swore to secrecy in order to maintain Dad's faith in me.

The very next day we were in the logging business. I had a good chainsaw now that I had purchased from Merland McLoud. We could cut logs and trees wood length and pull them out with Dolly. We did it a lot and Dolly soon wore out. She had the heaves and had to be pulled up onto her feet during her last days by block and tackle. It is not that the work was hard as most all the logs were pulled down hill, but Dolly was just too old. We were forced to use her less to a point where she was just an expense.

One day while piling our pulp beside the road a pickup truck came up the narrow dirt road and stopped. A red haired freckly man got out and walked up to me and said, "Hello, I'm Red Perkins. I had heard rumors about your job here and was curious enough to come over from Tamworth. You boys are cutting a lot of nice white birch." I told him we sold it to Ted Toby for paper pulp. He said, "Well you know if you were to sort out and stack the white birch separate in lengths of 39", 48" or 52" I could give you $50 a cord." I said, "We would be glad to do it but our horse is pretty weak and the good stuff is a longer haul now so it takes longer." Red came back with an answer right away. "Let me tell you about a friend of mine over in Maine. He has more horses for sale than you could ever dream of and they are all guaranteed too good for what you're doing. I'll take you over there in a week or so." With that he was gone. George and I talked it over and decided it was a good idea to get rid of Dolly.

Every Monday was the day for the livestock auction at Gray's in East Thetford, Vermont, so every Monday we would go over and see if we could find a horse dealer to come and pack Dolly up.

There were lots of dealers at this auction but one was a local man and he always had money and a reputation for buying everything and anything. I knew where his farm was in Plymouth, NH, near the Smith Covered bridge and along side Baker River. He was always referred to as Mule Skinner or Grubby Flanders. So I proceeded to get into a conversation with him about his son whom I was a classmate with prior to my Mother's death.

"You know Mr. Flanders, I have a white work horse that I am done using. She is a 16 hand mare and looks great, but is along in her years and I have to get something younger."

He said, "Well what are you looking to get for her?" I said, "$75 would be good, but for you $50 and you can come and get her tomorrow."

He said, "Sounds good, I'll pick her up tomorrow but you lead her down to the Stinson Lake Road, it's a lot easier for me to load her into my truck there."

We stayed and watched the auction, as I was always interested in auctions. Sometimes buying chickens, cows or whatever and then re-selling them a while later. The small animals were easy to transfer to NH; but cows, horses and such had to be checked by a vet.

We went home that afternoon where I was building myself a cabin near the barn where I could live by myself. It was midsummer and I could work long days to get a neat little cottage together from the salvage from other cottages at Eagle Point. It had a bedroom, living room and kitchen with insulation and wood walls made with matching boards. I had a wood kitchen stove that I made my own meals on and sparsely furnished with the necessities I picked up at auctions that I went to in the evenings.

Red Perkins showed up one day and we went to find a workhorse. We went to a stable in a little farm town in Southern Maine. Riding along with Red in his new pick up truck, he was telling me how he worked for a wood dowel making company in Westbrook, ME, called Saunders Brothers and they were now buying beech wood as well as white birch and I would be able to pay more for a horse because they would advance me the money in lieu of the wood. This sounded great to me and I was into getting a good horse. We were soon at the stable where we looked at twenty or more workhorses. I liked a large black mare and had it delivered the next day. The owner had said that he did not know a lot about her, only that he had heard she was a good pulling horse. The next day we put the old harness on this mare and went to work pulling out some of the logs which I had cut in the last week or so while we were without a horse. She could pull but did not obey commands and was always breaking loose and running off.

When Red came by to scale up our bolt wood, I told him this horse was no good and had to go. He was good about the situation and said this guy guaranteed all his horses so we would go right back up and pick a different one. We drove a couple of hours or so back to the stable and were greeted by the horse dealer. He did not seem surprised. He said, "I thought she might be a little wild for you, but she was in your budget and the better they are the bigger the price. You look around and we'll harness one up, because I do not want you to make the trip again unless the horse has an ailment or isn't sound."

I decided on "The Duke". He was large, yet short legged and stocky. He could work with no reins and responded to voice command. He looked great but had a weird mustache. The dealer said he had a funny face but was a great horse if I could afford him. He cost me more than my land, but I got a horse collar and new parts for my harness. In a couple of days the swap was made. Duke was a horse that everyone in the lumbering business around Ellsworth would talk about. He had great manners and could be trusted to do anything. He was a dark bay about 15.8 hands, large feet and very stocky. I could ride him up the mountain side and hook on two or three trees and he would take them to the landing and stand to be disconnected and go back for more. No need for reins to follow through the rough terrain.

I was finally making some money, working with the horse and my brother George every day. Sometimes Dad would come up and do what he could on the landing to help: disconnect Duke, or cut a tree in to make room for more.

My old $35 Chevy was soon having body rust problems and was taking a beating on the rough road. Dad's friend, Mr. Beckley, had a 1935 Ford Flat head VB, red with black fenders and chrome louvered hood which after a lot of negotiations, I was able to purchase for $35 and drive right home with temporary plates. It was a sharp old truck and I worked it hard everyday, trucking hay, lumber, wood and grain from Horace Bishop's Farm.

Summer was gone and fall was here. The mountains were in full bloom, the red maple, yellow poplar and birch and copper tone of the oak set the backdrop for a lot of artists and photographers. The leaf peepers were traveling all the back roads and enjoying the scenery. Hunting season was open and the out of state hunters were also around the lake a lot and searching for a place to set their tents to hunt or just camp out.

My logging operation was an attraction on the narrow dirt road around the back of Stinson Lake. There were large piles stacked by the roadside. With my great horse working by himself coming and going pulling large trees right down the road to piles where I would saw and stack piles four foot high along the road for hundreds of feet. There were large trucks sometimes blocking the road with noisy chain elevators, loading bolt wood to stack onto old 1940's logging trucks owned by truckers hired by Red Perkins and Toby Pulp Co.

It was not long before I was out of debt with the Sonders Brothers. As the Duke was paid off and I was buying things at auction to expand my little homestead.

It was fall, hunting season was open again. One day Ed Matuska stopped to watch my operation and visit. He inquired where he might set his tent for a few days. Ed was a worker at Smith's College in North Hampton, MA. I said, "Ed, I own all the land from the corner to the old logging landing, 1,000 feet or more down the road. Just pick out a spot to set up, no charge." The next day, Ed and his brother John were at my door. I invited them in and we visited a spell. He wanted to purchase a little piece of land from me where he could have a camp for vacations, but they did not have much money. I thought it over and said to give me a few days and I would think it over some more and come up with a plan.

A couple of days later, I had an opportunity to talk to an old friend, Mr. Bunker, the town clerk in Rumney, NH. He was an old timer who knew a lot about the real estate business. I told him that I owned my land free and clear and was thinking about selling some small lots off and taking back mortgages to make a bit of interest.

He said, "Albin, that's a great idea. Plan well, don't sell something you may need later and don't waste money on surveyors and lawyers and the like. Get a compass, measure off the lot and mark it with steel pipe or something more permanent measuring and writing down the direction for what you are selling. Come back and I'll show you how to write your deed and as far as the note and mortgage, I'll show you how to write a contract for a deed."

The next day I was up at the lumber lot with a compass and a long tape measure, planning a subdivision along a stretch of road frontage, but not too deep because I had a vision of doing lots behind the roadside lots. When Ed came the next week to camp again, I had a plan that Mr. Bunker had drafted on paper, lot location and size, a copy of proposed contract for deed with the lot description and location. Ed was very interested. He went to pick his lot right away. He got his brother John and other friends to contract for lots as well. The papers were signed and notarized and I was soon collecting monthly payments of $58 each. John was a couple of weeks late once and I told Ed, "Tell your brother John that I'm sorry, but a contract is just what is written and he has now null and voided the contract and the lot is for sale again."

Ed was coming up every weekend now, putting together a nice camp on his lot and making his payment very regularly. He, his wife and kids were great friends and they would stop by my cottage to visit for a spell and make payments. Ed also found someone to buy the lot that John had started to buy.

My sister, Maxine, and Clarence were in need of a home and they stopped by to talk to me about possibly getting a lot also. So I made a deal with them. I told them that they could work off the value of any lot they wanted and they set to work building a little house for themselves. Maxine had their son Junior and was expecting another child soon. They built a comfortable small home on the nearest lot to mine. It was not long before there was a half dozen cottages built in my new subdivision.

Cold weather was moving in and everyone was putting up firewood and winterizing their camps for the coming season. It was a long hard winter. I was lonely and I went to visit friends a lot as the logging had slowed due to the weather.

I went to the auction and bought a little Jersey cow for milk. She was a cute little cow and helped keep the Duke company in the barn. Maxine was due to have her second child in April and a cow would be handy.

The beautiful colors of fall had gone, and then the bare trees were covered with a blanket of snow. Sylvia and George were staying with Dad and Flora.

Everyone that could, went to Dad's house to celebrate Thanksgiving. It was a different get together than I was used to. Flora, Dad's wife, was much different than anyone I had lived with. She was kind of set in her ways although she always got along with Sylvia, who was now sixteen. John was staying there and that was a different story. He was only eight, but would retaliate many different ways, including putting Black Flag in her aquarium to kill her little guppies. He (in many ways) looked and acted like Dad would have in those circumstances.

It was near Christmas, so I decided to send a card and letter to Aunt Emaline just to let her know what was going on. I wrote a long letter apologizing for my not living up to their expectations and to tell them I was doing okay on my own. A few days later I received a note back saying that she was glad I was such a success but please do not move any of the mountains because she loved NH the way it was. I understood it and let it slide off like water on a duck's back. They were having a hard time and trying to sell the farm to relocate to NH.

Christmas came and went with little excitement. The Duke and Dolly the cow were my company morning and night. I would visit Maxine and my friends sometimes going to auctions or the Plymouth Theater. I was eighteen and my old classmates from Plymouth High were out evenings getting to enjoy the excitement of nightlife and exploring their sexuality. It was not that my hormones were not developed or working yet, but I never met anyone that I thought was compatible with me so I was going to wait.

Finally, it was April and the snow was melting. Maxine gave birth to her second child, Irene, named after our mother. The roads were very muddy and it was easy to become stuck with the pickup if you were not very careful to stay on well-packed ground. One evening a nice car with a couple in it drove by, heading around the back of the lake. I thought it odd, as the road was not passable to make it all the way around the lake due to the mud. The next thing I knew they were at my door. I recognized the lady right away; she was one of my classmates from high school. Her reputation was not the kind you would want for your daughter. She was famous for one-night stands. "Well, hello Albin, fancy meeting you here, what are you doing up here in the back woods?" she asked.

"Oh, I have lived here since high school ended last summer." I replied. She introduced me to her boyfriend and explained how they were out driving around and just happened onto my road and was attempting to turn around and their car sunk into the mud.

I walked a half-mile or so to take a look with them. The car was backed into an old turn around and just dropped to the floor in the spring mud. There was no way out other than to jack it up and build a road under it or pull it out. They had attempted to jack it up but the jack would only sink in the mud too.

I said, "I'm pretty sure I can get you out. I'll go harness up the Duke. You guys can wait and I'll be right back with the equipment." Duke was not being used a lot right now and was feeling his oats with it being spring and all. He was easy to harness and hook to the whiffle tree and chains. We walked down the road to the car where the heavy dodge car which was sunk in the mud.

In Duke's previous life he had been a competition horse for pulling in contests at fairs and the like. This had made him rather nervous when hooked to heavy loads. He acted as all horses do that are repeatedly used in pulling contests. He was eager to pull.

I turned him around and backed him to the front of the car. "You just hook the chain to your car and we'll give Duke a try.", I said, as I did not want to be responsible for any damage to his nice new car. So he hooked the chain around the heavy chrome bumper. All the time I was holding Duke's reins and backing him the last foot or two to connect to the whiffle tree. The minute he heard the chain connected, he was at the county fair in a pulling contest. He was nearly on his knees pulling until the bumper popped right off the car. They could not believe that the car was stuck so badly and that Duke could tear the bumper off. "Well," I said, "If you want him to try again you better find something a little more rugged to hook to this time and get into the car and try to help with turning the tires a bit." After some readjusting of the chains and equipment and connecting to the frame of the car we were ready to try Duke again.

He was still nervous and when the chain was hooked, he pulled sinking his feet into the mud until he was nearly on his knees. The car came flying out and onto solid ground. This was not the first or the last that the Duke was used to pull cars out of the mud, as it took a couple of weeks to dry out the roads in Ellsworth that spring.

It was an early spring in 1957, The muddy roads were drying out, the birds were back and the maples were budding. I was alone in my little house where I could dream and reminisce a lot. I was hearing Mom's voice from the past, "Keep your eye on the ball. Make up your mind what you would like in your life and work at it."

It was early morning and I had a good fire in the stove. I was going to make breakfast before going out for the day. The frying pan had a little too much bacon grease in it so I decided go to the door to dump it. While standing in the doorway, I reached out and held the pan in a position to pour the fat out. While holding the pan to drain, there was a loud crack from a rifle, and an instant hole through the pan. Raymond was walking up the road toward me and laughing in his unique "tee hee". In his way, he was showing me what a good marksman he was.

I was growing restless and had not made any money for a spell so I was entertaining the idea of job hunting or maybe finding a way to go on to college. Previously, after my eighteenth birthday I was at Clay's Newsstand in Plymouth, where I registered for the draft. Mr. Clay was a tall, large, stately man always friendly and willing to help anyone that walked into his paper store. He was a member of the local clubs and someone that I respected a lot. We had a conversation about the possibilities of getting further education and training through the military. I thought of this often that winter.

***

Now it was the first of May and things were still very slow, no jobs and no prospects. I wanted to meet new people and girls. Maybe learn a trade, something that was exciting and different. Good pay and respect. I gave the idea a lot of serious thought, I had tried farming and logging to no avail. I was ready to move on.

I went to Laconia to listen to recruiting officers for the Army, Navy and Air Force to see what they had to offer. The pay was small, but there were a lot of benefits and they were attractive to me at that time.

I was always interested in flying and travel was a great idea. Free medical insurance, free education, free clothes, free legal assistance to consummate my real estate business, room and board and thirty days paid vacation. It did not take long before I had talked myself into it. I talked it over with Clarence and Maxine. They agreed to care for my animals and sell them while I was away.

I agreed to enlist. I met again with the recruiter and went to Manchester for all kinds of tests and was excited and told I would be picked up in a week and taken to Grenior Air Field in Manchester. That evening I told Dad, Flora and the rest of the family. The response was not that good. Dad was very upset to think I would abandon my logging and lot selling business and go into the service. But as I told him, "There is no backing out now, I have already been sworn in and I am leaving in a couple of days."

Albert was still in Michigan working at the apple orchard with Ethel and his son. We wrote a little from time to time to fill each other in on what was going on with everyone. Jerry and Emmy were selling their stock and equipment and going to the Plymouth, NH area to live in the near future. Little Emmy was going back to live with Flora and Dad. I told him how I got tired of the down time in logging and I was longing for adventure, so I joined the Air Force. Dad was still having problems from his injuries from the Army and was struggling with his relationship with Flora. I promised to go see Albert as soon as I got some time off.

I left on May 27th, 1957 from Grennior Air Field in Manchester on a C47, a two prop engine plane with long wings, not really a passenger plane. There was a recruit from Keene, a golden glove boxer, a couple more loggers from the back woods and others from the Manchester area. All of us were 18 years old and just out of High School.

We were suppose to fly directly to Lackland Air Force base in San Antonio, Texas, but we ran into bad luck and one engine quit. Then a severe storm forced us to land in Shreveport, LA, where we stayed for a while. The plane was repaired and the weather cleared a bit allowing us to continue on our journey. We were taken by bus from where the plane landed to join many other enlisted personnel. We went through the same old routine with training instructors as all military. There were a few run-ins with the training instructors, but I did not see anything that our group could not handle. The sun was hot and at night we ran through the low lands with brush and small trees which were welcome as they were cooler. Wild yellow tomatoes were ripe and and hanging from the plants in the shaded low lands. We picked and ate them as we ran. The heat was intense after being accustomed to northern weather my whole life. We perspired a lot and were forced to take salt tablets. Our olive green fatigues turned white from the salt.

We all did KP (also known as kitchen detail) at least once and it was also used as punishment to anyone that fell short of the the training instructor's expectations. As time flew by, we trained in the heat of the early June sun. Although some big guys had problems from the heat

Me in the Air Force.

and had to be air lifted, my friends from New Hampshire and I had no problems.

To me and a few others, it was a Boy Scout camp with a lot of hiking, marching, camping and war games like some teenagers do. It was more fun than we had anticipated. After a month or so, we tested to see what jobs we were best suited for. Then we would be sent to the school where we were most needed. John and I ended up going to Chanute Technical School in Rantoul, Ill.

It was not what I was looking forward to, but I knew it was going to be another adventure. At Chanute things were different. I had weekends off and could go off base as long as I was in for bed check on Sunday night by 9:00 p.m. My MO or new career was to be an aircraft electrical technician. The course took a minimum of six months and longer if you did not pass. I soon met many new friends and everyone was involved in drinking, girls and having a good time whenever they had a free pass. The little town of Rantoul was known for its red light district and other activities to keep the military men broke. John, myself and some other boys were into getting far away from base on our days off.

Albert was still in Michigan, so one Friday night after school I went to the barrack, showered, and dressed in class A uniform and hitchhiked north to Michigan. It was so easy. I would only have to stick my thumb out and the first car to come along would pick me up, sometimes for a short ride and other times for 100 miles or more.

Upon reaching Michigan that night, I borrowed Albert's old 148 Chevy Coupe and toured around. I went to see my old friend Frank and others. I was having a great time. I did this several times. It was so good that I could hitchhike back and forth regularly and not be late getting back to the base in most cases. If anyone was late, the other guys in the barracks would cover for them. We would roll up the mattress and bedding of all the guys who were not back in time and tell the bed check personnel that they had all shipped out. It was simple and it worked.

One night I returned late. My bed was rolled and the bed check was to come in right away, so I went to a storage room and climbed up on top of a rack of toolboxes where I was so tired I fell asleep. I rolled over, fell off the top shelf and bounced off every shelf on my way down to the concrete floor below. I was bruised, but did no serious damage.

Sometimes during Phys Ed. Class the next morning friends were covering for missing guys who had not made it back yet by responding to roll call for them. I had a friend from Grand Rapids, Don Johnson, he was a bit slow, but a great friend. The TI (training instructor) was calling roll one morning. After Don had already covered for one missing buddy. The TI called, "John Jossalyn" and Don responded loudly "Yes, Sir". Then the TI Called, "Don Johnson" and Don responds again, "Yes, Sir." The TI recognizing the same voice looked at him and said, "So who the hell are you?" "Don Johnson, Sir." " So where is John Jossalyn?"

Without a second thought, Don replied, "Shipped out Sir and I thought you said, Don Johnson, Sir." It was a close call but everything went over okay. When John showed up later he was told of the roll call problem. He was later discovered by the TI and ended up with 2 week KP Duty.

I was still doing my real estate lot sales and receiving payments from them. I got free legal aid form Air Force attorneys and was closing on some lots. So I decided to buy a 1950 Ford Police car. It was painted up like a police car, but it had a big flathead VB engine and could really move out.

It took a while to get it on the road, but I was still hitchhiking to Michigan weekly and having crazy experiences every week. John went with me one week to a little street fair in Belding where I had gone to High School. We met a couple of girls as we were walking the streets. I got the number and address of Patricia Beemer of Lowell, Michigan. We visited for a while and I said I might be back up sometime this next weekend.

John and I hitchhiked to Grand Rapids and rode back with Don Johnson. He had an old Dodge. It was sometimes worse than hitchhiking. It burned oil badly and was hard to start. So it did not make the trip more than a couple of times.

School was going along fine but the summer days were hot in the metal buildings on the flight lines. I always looked forward to the weekends and free time from the Air Force Base.

The next weekend I hitchhiked to Lowell, MI where I walked the three miles of dirt road to Patricia's home. It was a narrow farm road to a small duplex. Her mother, Violet, and three teenagers lived on one side and her grandmother and grandfather on the other side. We visited for a while and her grandfather took me for a short drive to help me hitchhike back. The next weekend I returned with my own car and I made the trip weekly with it for a while.

I found the school very interesting and the fundamentals of electricity came fairly easy to me. Aircraft electrics are a little more tricky than household electrics as aircrafts use both DC with battery storage and AC from alternators, not generators.

We covered all aspects of electricity, and the different components used in aircrafts. I found it interesting and never missed a day, but when time off came, I was off that base.

I always tried to go north to Michigan on my time off. I traveled many different routes. One time while hitchhiking back to base along Lake Michigan, I was walking along the highway attempting to catch a ride in sparse traffic when a new white Cadillac came flying down the road. I extended my thumb in an attempt to catch a ride in this flying car. The driver came to a screeching stop, yelling, "Come on! Come on! Get in here!" I hastily jumped in and we were pulling out before the door was closed. The driver was a rather large man in a western wide brim hat. He was pushing his new white Cadillac convertible to the limits. While flying along on Lakeshore Drive he says, "Hey boy, you see that little plane up there? Well, that's my dumb wife. She thinks she can beat me to Chicago. Well, I'll show her!" I never did find out who won, but I know I was some glad when he came to a stop and I bailed out.

On another occasion, I was hiking up the Toledo Detroit expressway when a young couple stopped and picked me up with their brand new 1957 Plymouth Fury. The car was advanced for the time. It had high rear fender fins, a large V8 engine and all the extras. Cars were traveling along at a good speed, but we were passing everyone, gaining more and more speed. The telephone poles began to look like a picket fence. The lady was covering her face and screaming and the driver was yelling angrily, "They promised me this thing would do 135 mph no problem and I'm having a hard time getting over 125." 1955 through 1959 was a time for big muscle cars, but I was from an age where cars that went up to 80 mph were over the top. At 125 I was definitely a believer and I was praying for a soft landing. When we came to a stop near Dearborn, I got out and thanked God for the speedy trip and safe landing.

I went to Patricia's house every weekend that I could and called her once in a while. We were getting along very well and sometimes we went out on the town when I had my car up there. Her mother, Violet, was a strict Christian and did not want us to stay out very late.

After a short few months of courtship Patricia and I were engaged and were making plans for our wedding. I visited her family every time I could. We drove to New York City and New Hampshire where I introduced her to my family.

It was a cold January day and we were married in a small church near Lowell, Michigan. Frank was my best man. Patricia's friends made up the rest of ushers, bridesmaids and so on. Things went quite smoothly. I took my vows before a Baptist minister and was happy to think that I had found a mate for life. The vows were repeated by Patricia and I, however they did not really mean much at the time.

That night was short, as we were to take a bus early the next morning to Maguire Airforce Base. I had made arrangements for us to stay at a friend's house until we could get a place of our own.

That ride on the bus the morning after marrying Patricia would prove to be an education. I was ready to call it quits. The ride was long and I was seeing a different side of my new wife. I did my best to see her side of this new life for her and I did all I could to make her happy.

My friend had a little room with a small bed which he let us use for a hundred dollars. The bed had a layer of newspaper under the mattress. Patricia was very embarrassed by the sound of the paper every time we moved in the bed. Therefore, sex was out of the question.

We looked desperately for anything to rent to get out of my friend's house. After a couple of weeks I was able to find a small bungalow in New Egypt where we managed to live for less than the hundred it cost at my friend's. Now we had privacy and the new found joy of sex was reason to overlook the nagging and all the other things about Patricia that were driving me crazy.

The air force was only paying me thirty nine dollars every two weeks and it was hard to make ends meet, but I was able to use some of my savings and sell more lots in New Hampshire to get by.

It was not long with all our unprotected sex, Patricia was pregnant. She seemed to be more content in this condition than she had been since we were married.

I worked many jobs in my spare time to make ends meet. Landscape work, grocery store stock and warehouse work and furniture deliveries were just a few of the jobs that I did to make ends meet. All this work to make a life for Patricia and our unborn child was keeping me busy both night and day. I was an electrician at night for passenger planes at McGuire and a truck driver for a furniture store days. The idea of becoming someone was now put on the back burner. Now it was a struggle just to support myself and my growing family.

I was really lucky compared to many others as I was able to find work to supplement my military pay. While rushing from job to job early one morning, in a 1950 Studebaker, I went around a corner too fast on wet pavement. The car went into a fishtail and I could not keep the car on all four wheels. The car hit the dirt as it spun around sideways. As soon as the tires hit the dirt on the side of the road, it rolled over onto it's roof. It spun around on its roof with a loud noise and slid over a cable guard rail and down into a swamp where it finally came to a stop. With the wheels still turning, I managed to crawl out a window and get back onto the road just as a large yellow bus came around the corner.

The bus came to a stop and a group of migrate workers, who were picking pickle cucumbers in the area, got out and rolled the car over onto its wheels. They then pushed the car into the road where I started it and drove on to my next job. I did take the time to thank the group of men that helped me that day and vowed to do the same for others if the time ever came that I was needed.

At work, I excused myself for being a bit late and told my boss of my mishap. He took it as a wisecrack and did not believe me. So finally, I said, "Come take a look at the car." The door handles were broken off, the roof was dented and had deep scratches from the cable guard rail. The tail lights were broken and the car was a mess. He was shocked. "Boy, I do not know how you managed to do this and not get hurt."

After a week or so of driving the beat up car back and forth to work I managed to talk some friends into going to a junk yard for parts. We got some "Bonda" and put the car into the Air Force body shop. A week later, it was looking great and ready to swap in on a 1956 Thunderbird. What a transition! It was not your ordinary family car, but it was the only fun car in my life. For this, I was willing to make payments.

Times were hard. I would go to the mess hall to eat and take food home for Patricia when we did not have money enough to buy a can of tuna. When I was not able to afford the price of a Christmas tree, a friend from the base came dragging one in that he had requisitioned from someone's lawn, lights and all.

We had tried to sublet part of the house to a fellow air man and his fourteen year old wife. Fred Hobbs and his wife were from the hills of Kentucky. Fred had told us that he had rescued her from physical and sexual abuse from her brothers. And now they were in need of temporary housing like Patricia and I when we were fist married. Fred had told me stories about his new bride and her family and how he had sent her a ticket to come by bus to Trenton. We were to go pick her up there one afternoon. Fred and I were there waiting when the bus pulled in and passengers began to depart the bus. Now in my mind I am visualizing a poor fourteen year old immature long haired girl. Boy was I off. When Fred identified a tall, over endowed blond, who looked twenty as his wife, I must have looked shocked.

"Yes, that's her." He assured me.

We managed to live together for a few weeks before Patricia and the young Kentucky bride had some harsh words and they were looking for new housing.

***

It was January of 1959, Friday the 13th, and Patricia gave birth to our first son, Gerald Allen. We had moved to a better little house in Hornerstown where we had room to have a garden and a room for the baby. Patricia's sisters would come to visit from time to time and we went to New Hampshire sometimes to visit my family whenever we could. Other than for those little breaks, I worked every day and night to support my family.

I had sold the balance of my subdivision to supplement my income, which was still only thirty nine dollars every two weeks from the air force plus what I managed to make driving a truck, which was not enough to keep everyone happy.

The military was not raising anyone's rank or rate of pay and it was hard to make ends meet. So I decided that I would leave the Air Force and try to do better back in New Hampshire working a better paying job.

The old log home was Maxine and Clarence's home for a while back in the 50's and Dad had moved another one in from Stinson Lake for him and his new bride to live in.

Flora moved back to her home on river street in Holderness, just across the bridge from Plymouth, Main Street.

I went to Dad's house on route 118 in Dorchester New Hampshire to make a friendly visit. We showed off our new son and listened to Dad tell me what I should be doing with my life.

The house which was moved from Stinson Lake to Ellsworth burned in 1955. Dad sold the property and purchased a small run down farm in Dorchester. My sister and brother, Little Emmy and John, were staying with him here for a while. Dad was courting a lady (Margaret Quimby) across the street. She ran the Dorchester Diner and Dad ate there regularly.

Dad's little farm had a small barn on a couple acres of land with a small brook meandering through it. It was here that I sat down with my wife and baby to discuss our future. Dad was trying to convince me to buy a small house on North Dorchester Road and work in the woods to pay my bills and purchase the house. It was not much of a plan and it was not what I wanted to do with my life. However, it seemed like a starting point. Patricia and I thought it would be a better life than New Jersey life, so we made the move.

The house was very remote and in desperate need of repairs. The floors were sagging toward a chimney in the center of the living room and the rest of the floors were nearly as bad. There was no heating system and minimal utilities.

I took a temporary job at a mill in Plymouth, making shoe shanks. I worked there with schoolmates from my early days and had a lot of fun, but was not paid well. It was a long trip to work every day and the house in northern Dorchester was not livable in the winter so we moved to a rental in Plymouth.

Ralph Batchelder, a friend from my childhood days back in Ellsworth, was working with me. He was the youngest son of the Batchelder family. He, his brothers and sister (Bertha) went to school with me and my siblings at the little red schoolhouse in West Campton during the Second World War. We had a blast working together; swinging from crane cables, playing jokes on fellow employees and just terrorizing the place.

I would do the jobs that no one else would. Therefore, I was working on the crane at sub zero weather doing repairs, running a de-barker, stacking wood in a steam room and countless other bad jobs. The foreman, Robert Little liked me a lot because of this, he had tolerated all of my hell raising. One day while working in the steamroom I was stacking wood blocks, which were being cut from logs by a large saw. The blocks would drop from the swing saw onto a chute and slide into the steam room where I would stack them. These blocks of wood were coming at a fast pace, as fast as the saw man could cut them. In order to keep up I was stacking fast and took a large block from the chute which I could not lift. It dropped to the concrete floor and bounced against the concrete wall with my hand between it and the wall. The impact took off four finger nails and cut open the pads of my fingers.

I was sent down the street to a doctor's office where I met young Doctor Henry Crane. He listened to my story as I sat in an old arm chair across from him. With my hand on the arm of the chair and Doctor Crane asking me how my hand was feeling he reached over and quickly removed a hanging finger nail. He medicated and dressed my hand and I returned to work.

It was not long before I was called to the office to be reprimanded for some practical joke I had done on an older employee. I told Robert Little that it would not happen again and was going to be out of his hair. I thanked him for his help with the job and told him I was going to work at the Lincoln Paper Mill where the pay was better.

I was still driving my '56 Ford and doing all the side jobs that I could find time for. I ran into and old neighbor from the 1940's who owned a shingle and window shop in West Campton. Arthur Moulton was a clever old man that ran his little mill on water power and sometimes a flat belt drive from an old 1819 Buick engine. Because of my electric training, he hired me to wire his mill and paid me one dollar per foot to dig a frost-free ditch and bury a copper water line. The line ran from high on a hill across the road and brook to his home.

It was no easy task; a stone lined, hand dug well was the beginning point. It was all down hill from there. Under tree roots, around and under rocks, down steep inclines, across Branch Brook (down stream) and up to a water barrel in Arthur's kitchen. It was a test of persistence which proved to be rewarding.

Arthur had a daughter named Marion, she was a bit older than I was and had built a new home up the road a couple of miles or so with a former husband. She was very outgoing and was always looking for a man, but that's another story.

I managed to talk her into selling me her new home for little money. In order to finance the purchase I sold my Ford and got a mortgage at Plymouth Bank. This was my first dealing with Ken Bartlett the president. Who wanted you to know he was president. "Hey kid how ya' gonna pay for this?"

We moved to West Campton where I worked at the paper mill and did odd jobs for a while. I was working at Giggs' auction hall in Rumney every Saturday night as a runner and sometimes auctioneer. This was my passion. I just loved it. I could entertain and I could sell anything. Maybe this was what I was searching for. The job at the paper mill was hard, poling logs in the pond and feeding the chipper. The young trench workers from Canada were hard to get along with and I was looking to move up. The house in West Campton was a small cape with a large wood furnace, which kept it cozy without a lot of effort. I was always improving it and finishing off unfinished rooms, putting in dormer windows and expanding the upper level, etc.

Patricia was pregnant with the our second son and the push was on to make more money. Marion Moulton was working at a lamp factory, housed in the old Plymouth railroad station. Her employer just so happened to be building a new house down the street from me and was interested in me and my work ethics. He asked Marion to tell me he had some work for me and to drop by some morning on the way to work at the mill. I met Norman Perry the next day and went to work for him at his house only a quarter of a mile down the road from my house.

Milton Davis was a car dealer in Woodstock and he had a reputation for selling cheap used automobiles. I became a good customer of his as I was always fixing one up in the garage under our home. I had about every make of automobile in that basement at one time or another. While up to Milty's with a friend one day, we were given the tour of all of his great treasures in his expansive yard.

"…and this 1955 Plymouth is a gem. I picked it up in Acton, Mass. the other day. Drove it all the way back. Runs great and never used a drop of oil." The tow bar was still hooked to the front bumper.

Before we left Bing was talked into buying an Oldsmobile and I bought an old Studebaker pickzup for twenty five dollars. Bing borrowed a plate and we left. I was to return in a day or so with a tow bar to pick up the Studebaker. A few days later Bing told me the Oldsmobile engine had thrown a rod or something, so he was looking to return it to Milty.

I said "Not a problem, I have the tow bar so I can take it back and pick up the Studebaker at the same time." We pulled into the yard and were greeted by Milty.

"What can I do for you guys today?"

Bing said, "Well this Plymouth is a damn lemon. The engine went in it before I could get it home and it has a lot of other major problems. Maybe we could renegotiate the price." Milty without hesitation or sign of anger or disappointment replied, "Park it right over there under the tree and another Bing Rogers will come right along."

I worked for Norman Perry and his alcoholic wife for a short time at their home and then became a full-time foreman at their lamp factory in Plymouth. The business grew and I worked long hours for two dollars an hour. I was soon promoted and was in charge of all production and shipping. For that responsibility I got another ten cents an hour. I liked the business a lot and developed some fixtures and tools to speed up production, but it was a bit like the farm work back in Michigan. I was struggling to keep the wolf away from the door and I did not feel that I was appreciated.

Time was flying by in my life, I would frequently think of all the talks that I had with my mother. "Make up your mind what you want do with your life while here on earth. You are only here for a short time." She had always had expectations of greater achievements in me and shared enthusiasm when I did well and disappointment when I fell short of her expectations. Mom had many little sayings that used to guide me through life and I often apply them to help guide me through life still.

***

Patricia had given birth to our second son Christopher, it was April of 1961 and our family life was not doing well. She was always in demand for more from me.

I was working at every auction that I could and trying to develop my own style of auctioneering which everyone liked. I practiced my chant while driving to my day job most every day. At every sale I worked, I was told by the public how they enjoyed the work that I was doing and encouraged me to open my own place for commission sales. Maybe this was to be my profession.

Sylvia and Joe would visit from time to time and she was talking about a barn for sale in Thornton where I could run auction sales. After following up on this lead I found an old cattle barn run down and just packed with trash, hay and rot.

I bought the barn and land for six hundred dollars from a neighbor lady that just wanted me there to run auctions.

I had to get a license to operate auctions which was not hard as I had plenty of friends that were willing to help me get the affidavits showing my good business judgement and bonds, etc., but getting the barn and the parking lot ready for a scheduled August opening was a real struggle. I hired local kids and a friend, Bob Hoyt, to remove all of the trash and throw it into a ravine on the property. I worked every minute that I could to get the barn cleaned and renovated so as to conduct an auction by the middle of August.

The barn was close to the road with two large sliding doors opening onto Route #3, the main highway from Boston to Canada. The siding was old weathered clapboards with holes where manure was piled out windows years before. Bobby Hoyt and I would load a large tarp with hay and debris, then drag it to a nearby deep ravine where we dumped the load and returned for more. Bobby was a good friend and talked a lot while we worked all day. He had problems with his women friends and it came up frequently in our conversations.

I was successful in getting my license and running my first commission sale in August of 1963. I conducted sales every Saturday night and tried to come up with different ideas to entertain as well as to sell. I always greeted the crowd and told them the rules that I followed to run my sales. They were simple and short. One of the rules forbid anyone from smoking in the barn. This was a hard rule to enforce in the early 1960's, but I was determined to eliminate any smoke in my barn for health and fire reasons. If I were auctioneering and someone lit a cigarette, the smoke would find me and compromise my voice. To handle this situation I would stop my sale and announce, "Someone out there is smoking and I will be glad to continue once it is put out." In a few minutes I would continue my chant.

"We have here what looks like a blown glass ink well. It very well could be one of a kind and what am I bid?"

"50 bidder the 75 and would you now go the dollar sir?"

"Yes it's your turn and now one and a quarter ma'am and a half sir don't go home and wished you had."

"Do I have one and quarter, going, going, going, gone. And what do you know I just found another one just like it ma'am, make it a matched pair another dollar and a quarter. The buyer takes 2 on number 56."

This was a kind of practical joke that I did from time to time. There was a case of 48 inkwells under my auction bench where I housed items to sell when I was not supplied with a new item from the consignors. It kept the auction going and I would continue my sale, selling without interruption for hours. Sticking a joke in from time to time and greeting someone as I sold an item. I sold everything from household items, antiques, livestock, construction equipment and supplies to complete estates.

I was still working at the lamp factory. I was eager (as always) to better myself and always looking for a better job with more money. McMillan Construction Company was building a new girls dormitory, the Pemigewasset Hall, at Plymouth State College and was looking for help. So I gave my notice at the lamp factory and signed on for McMillan. The notice was not well taken by the Perry's and they hired a lawyer to try to force me to stay employed by them. The lawyer told them that I was a free agent and just because they had salaried me did in no way compel me to stay in their employment.

Their effort was in vain. I went to work for McMillan right away. I was soon doing payroll, tracking the time the construction workers were on the job and what they were doing and calculating their pay checks. I did a lot of different jobs for them. Some as far away as Keene and Rindge, New Hampshire.

On March 29th of 1964, Patricia gave birth to our third son, Tate. I was a proud father and Patricia was a great mother. We were the ideal family, envied by many people.

We made it through the cold winters, burning wood to stay warm and working spare time to make another room in the house. The cost was more than I could bare.

The auctions were still doing well in the summers but were hard in the winter without a good heating system. I was still getting visits from Mom in the dead of night, "Make up your mind what you want out of life and work at it." Well, I guess this was it. I loved to auctioneer. People loved and encouraged me. I always had fun with it, even though it was not that profitable. So I was always trying to upgrade the barn to encourage more business and to look more professional.

We had moved into a little house up the road, north of the Auction Barn. The house was small and needed work. I negotiated a deal with the owner to rent to own. After work I put in a heating system and upgraded the house some.

Patricia was pregnant and I was looking for a daughter. I had told everyone that I was not going to shave until I got one. On July 13, 1966 Patricia gave birth to a much wanted daughter, Victoria.

While working for McMillan in Plymouth a few months later, I overheard a conversation between a couple of carpenters about a project in Waterville, NH. I was working long hours and driving sometimes over one hundred miles each day to work for $2.70 per hour. And a carpenter job just up the road a bit for $4.26 was really attractive. This was an opportunity I just could not pass up.

It was a cold fall day the latter part of September 1966, I drove up the Waterville Valley Road along side Mad River. It was overcast and raining lightly. The fall leaves had mostly fallen and it was a raw cold day to go looking for a job.

After some time, driving through a long, rough, muddy road under construction, I reached a site with a construction trailer and equipment around an excavation site and the start of concrete foundation work. I got out of my pickup and was walking through the mud to an office trailer and a short middle aged man with a military persona opened the door and asked me who I was looking for.

"My name is Albin Conkey and I have come to work as a carpenter on the base lodge." And with a quick response he said, "Well, I'm Sunney Wilson, the foreman, and if you are working here you better get with it. The prints are on the table and all the concrete forms are right there." I had little experience with form work, but knew I could follow anyone else. I knew I was early to work, but after an hour or so I realized I was the whole crew for that day. The work was hard, cold and muddy, but the money was nearly twice what I had ever made. The next day, I met more men who had shown up for the higher paying jobs. There was a variety of workers running around doing their best at a job which they knew very little about. The super was a tall thin no nonsense frenchman, Al LaVassa, who spent much of his time stringing bows for deer hunting.

***

The weather was less than desirable, lots of snow, cold and windy, yet we worked long days. And the work crew grew to around a hundred or more. Carpenters and tradesmen to construct the base lodge and all of the buildings necessary to run the Waterville Valley ski area.

I worked here for a couple of years doing many different jobs in the construction field as well as grooming the slopes and making snow.

I had my brothers, Albert, George, Raymond and John working here on the Waterville project with me. It was a blast. Literally, Raymond was drilling and blowing all the rocks that were a problem on the J bar slope. He would scream his warning "fire in the hole" many times to no avail or response. When he detonated the charges at lunch break, the air was full of falling stones of all sizes.

I was in Brother John's Oldsmobile, having a sandwich and sharing conversation way down in the parking lot, when the stones started to bounce off the car, John was cursing and getting his car out of there as soon as possible. The falling stone did damage to parked vehicles, buildings and equipment, but Thumper defended Raymond for this over blasting. He pointed out the signs posted at the entrance to Waterville, stating that this was a blasting area and to enter at your own risk. There was some arguing and threats of legal repercussions, however it was fruitless.

My brothers were traveling a pretty good distance from Dorchester to work. And most times using the back road through Ellsworth, it was shorter and a good chance to shoot deer. Raymond was so successful he was eating venison three meals a day. In fact, he smelled like a deer.

They were working on roads and tower foundations where they were being supervised by Thumper Bixby. Thumper was a radical that was into getting the job done no matter what. They worked long hours and did the impossible with little to work with. When he needed culverts, lumber or anything which he could not get fast through a supply company, he would ask them to get it any way they could. They were known to remove major items (culverts and the like) from other jobs to use on Thumper's jobs. He made reference to them as his requisition crew.

In turn they were rewarded with booze and additional hours on their time cards. They constructed concrete tower bases where the ground was too steep to stand and when asked how they did it, they would credit it to the booze.

When the construction work ran out we remained there in the ski area and worked for the resort maintaining slopes and making snow.

We all drove the Tucker snow cats, grooming the trails night after night. They were easy to operate and kind of fun, however there were some white knuckle experiences while trying to traverse the steep slopes in white out conditions. George totaled one when he was crossing a slope and slid down the slope and crashed into a tower. Brother John was working the welcome trolley and always carried a bottle. He was being chased by ski bunnies to share it with. He was to be a marine in Vietnam only days later.

I worked on other projects, The Outlook, Davis's Lodge, Paul Phosi's Lodge, The Four Seasons Restaurant and many small jobs. I had my own crew and we worked together to get jobs done fast.

The auctions were going gang busters. Every Saturday night the barn was standing room only and truck loads of consignments were lined up at the back door.

I moved a cottage from the Wonderland Village down the road a few miles, and put it on a foundation behind the auction barn and on the banks of Hubbard Brook. It was positioned to take advantage of the view, looking north across the brook and up the Pemigewasset River valley. I also had employed Bing Rogers (a close friend whom had done all the stone work in Waterville) to make a large retaining wall around the house. He also constructed a large L shaped swimming pool between the house and the brook.

I managed to sell the house that we were living in and move into the cottage by the Auction Barn. It was small, but everyone had their own room for the first time.

The barn was not large enough to accommodate the large crowds and I was forced to build on. I put on a second floor to keep the heat down in the winter months. Raymond helped cut timbers from an old three story barn at the Butternut Farm in West Campton. We trucked loads of boards and timbers from there to the auction barn, where I started the task of making a second floor.

Sylvia stopped by and helped with handling timbers and boards a couple of days. She was rugged and good help. She had worked on most places that she had lived in and had knowledge of the building trade. During those times we talked of the good old times and shared our frustrations with life and the problems at present. She complained about her married life. It was bad. I understood, as my marriage was not going well either. So we compared notes as we lifted large timbers into place to support a second floor.

***

Maxine and her family would come to the auctions to visit and sometimes help keep books. She, her husband (Clarence), son Junior now 12, daughter Irene, and son Gary were living in a house on Route #175 in Holderness. They had befriended Blacky Martel, a man from Giggs auction hall years ago. He helped Maxine get this house to rent. He was a short dark haired whiskery man always talking about making it big. He dressed in dark clothes and appeared greasy as an auto mechanic.

One day Blacky came to their house to take Maxine and Clarence to shop or visit. He unloaded his truck to make room for them to get in. They put the guns, coats, and stuff in the house from a previous hunting trip, and left the three kids to fend for themselves. In their absence a shot gun was taken from the coffee table where it was left. One of Irene's brothers picked up the weapon and discharged it taking Irene's life in a most brutal manner. She was only eleven and the victim of ignorance. To this day I do not keep guns in my house because of this act of carelessness. The loss to Maxine was so great, that she never bore more children and could not ever talk of the incident for the rest of her life. Blacky came to my sales from time to time, but I tried to avoid him.

***

I worked day jobs and worked at remodeling the barn, rebuilding the cottage and collecting items for the weekly auctions. I was doing some outside estate auctions where I needed a large canvas tent. I drove to the Eureka factory in Binghamton, New York where I purchased one. It was a red and white striped party top. I used it at most all my outside auctions and it was not long before someone was wanting to borrow it for a wedding.

Because I was concerned about getting the top dirty or damaged, I agreed to loan it but I would have to get $50 for labor to set it up and take it down. The demand grew and I was forced to buy more tents of many sizes and require reservations. The tent rental business was a great cash income from March until the first snow fall. A lot of the business was repeat business for clubs, schools, ski areas and the such. I required a 50% payment at the time of reservation and cash balance at the time the tent was erected. Waterville, now being called Waterville Valley, always had a spring clam bake and reserved a large tent for the occasion. From past experience, I was aware of their bad credit and payment record. When I went to set the tent at the upper end of the golf course there was a few spectators but no one with the balance of the rental fee. After a short wait, I decided to load the few things which were laying on the ground in preparation to leave.

A man stepped up and said, "What are you doing?"

I replied, "Well I have a signed written agreement requiring full payment in cash before the tent is set up and Waterville Valley has a bad reputation when it comes to paying their bills. I am here and the money is not. I cannot wait any longer."

The man said, "Well I know the person who rented the tent and I will put the money up for him."

I replied, "Thank You. We will get it right up then."

As a rule the tent rental business was trouble-free and helped pay bills made by other activities in my life. My sons and I got real good at setting tents and would compete at setting tents where multiple tents were required, such as fairs and the like. While at the Plymouth Fair, we set a 40 foot tent in 20 minutes next to what was to be a girly strip show.

They were attempting to set a tent of equal size, but they were not experienced in setting tents. We had our tent up and we were resting on the ground, watching them unload their tent. They had not even started yet.

The lady next door, from whom I had purchased my barn, had sold her house to Fred and Nelly Adams, an older couple from down the road a piece. Fred was a loyal customer at my sales every week. The auctions were bringing large crowds, but it did not net a lot of money. Dad and Margaret were always there, sometimes bookkeeping or consigning something. He also would come to air some problem with me, in hopes of getting me to solve his problems.

His cottage, which came from the same place as my home, was located on someone else's land by a few feet. He was looking to solve the problem; and I guess he did as it burned shortly thereafter.

Dad married Margaret at a double wedding with my sister, Emaline and Howard, at the Dorchester Diner, the former home of Margaret. It was a fairly nice home with a front room devoted to dining for the public. It was small, cozy and warm for the locals. It made a living for her and her daughter.

Dad had a small farm across the way and had sold it to my brother George, retaining a small lot on the other side of a stream which divided the property. This lot was where they had put their cottage after Margaret sold the diner to her daughter. Dad pulled in an old trailer and built an addition onto it where they lived. He raised a garden along the brook and kept a fierce mongrel hound dog and a large cat. Neither one were to be trusted. They would bite and Dad had to control them whenever one came to visit. Dad raised vegetables and flowers and brought them to the auctions weekly to sell. The auction barn was a great place for gossip and conversations.

People would talk politics, economics, news and just anything that was on their mind at the time. It was a lot like Grandpa Albert's front porch so many years ago. Fred was complaining about the town taxing all cattle the same whether they were worth ten dollars a head or fifty dollars. Others shared my discontent of high property tax.

There were other issues in town management that got me interested in changing things.

Fred came by to convince me that I should run for town selectman, a thankless, time consuming job. So in preparation I voiced my opinion at the auctions and went door to door to selected voters and Fred did the same.

A few days later in March of 1968, the town of Thornton had their annual meeting. There were three candidates for the office of selectman, of which I was one. After the meeting the supervisors, veteran selectmen, other candidates, and people gathered around to wait for the outcome or tally from all the votes.

I was considered an outsider and not a true contender as I had not been active in town politics or even lived in the town that long. Conversations which I overheard between the other selectmen and another candidate for the job had pretty much discounted me from being the new selectman.

When the votes were finally tallied I was tied with their favored candidate. The officers were not sure how to solve this outcome and postponed the swearing in until they had consulted the secretary of state. A couple of days later the problem was solved. The town clerk was to draw a name from a hat. Old Jim Pope was all smiles when he drew my name and congratulated me. He was a great friend for the rest of his life.

Me winning the tie vote.

    I worked at the auction on weekends, did construction work during the weekdays, and rented tents at night when possible. I was still struggling to make ends meet and to be the person I thought I should be. It is not always easy to do the things you enjoy and supply things that everyone else needs to be happy; it becomes a financial and stressful position to endure.

    Patricia was much easier to be around when she was pregnant and I took advantage of that.

    On November 13, 1968, Patricia gave birth to our fourth son, Jeff. He was an easy baby to raise. The other children were growing up fast and he benefited from all the things we had learned from his siblings.

    Al Moulton, an electrician from Massachusetts, had invested in property on the Upper Mad River Road and was preparing to build a complex called The Waterville Valley Gateway. I met with him and we formed a relationship that lasted for years. I had a crew of more than forty workers. We could put together buildings at remarkable speed. We built all of the condominiums and the many amenities in record time and for little money. While working for him I lost sight in my right eye, broke my back, leg and other bones. I constructed many houses and commercial buildings for him and other people. All the time in search of what I could do to make the big mark in life.

Time flew by, I had put six studio apartments on the top of the auction barn where Sylvia and I had put that second floor. It was difficult to keep the construction crew busy during slow times and to help cash flow. There were a lot of different people that rented those apartments and some became very good friends. Danny Coehlo was a good example. I went to Italy with him and friends and he has visited me many times since. I bought a motel at the Jack O' Lantern Resort and moved it to the property adjacent to the auction barn where I rented rooms.

While running the auctions I made many, many friends. There were all kinds of people from everywhere. Consignors were coming weekly from Rhode Island, Vermont, Massachusetts and every place imaginable. It was hard for me to go anywhere without bumping into a friend or at least someone that I knew.

While on a trip to Italy one fall with my good friend Dan Coehlo, I ran into a lady from Dorchester, New Hampshire. She was a neighbor of Dad and she thought that I was sent by her husband to spy on her in Venice. What a small world. I explained why I was there and we parted on good terms.

The sheriff, Herb Ash was a regular. He was a military buddy of Dad. Herb had lost one leg while serving in the second world war and had an artificial one, which he got around on very well. Whenever I had trouble collecting on a bad check, Herb would take the check and come to the next sale with the money. Once I had a bad check given to me from a buyer in Vermont across the river from Woodsville, NH and out of jurisdiction of a Grafton County Sheriff. Herb said, "It may take a little longer, but I'll get it." A few days later, Herb heard that Frank Nutter was running a sale in Woodsville. Knowing that this guy could not pass up an auction, Herb had a friend of his talk to the unsuspecting maker of the bad check. Herb's friend told him of the upcoming sale. On the day of the sale, Herb was there early and waited for the culprit to show up. Herb met the maker of the bad check as he entered the auction hall. Herb said "Hi, I'm Herb Ash I'm the sheriff of Grafton County and I'm here to collect the cash from you for this check." As he held the check out for inspection, the man tried to make promises to cover the check later.

He said, "I will get down to the Thornton Auction Barn and pay for it at their next sale." Herb replied "No, I do not think so. You will give me the money right now or you will end up down the street in the jail. You have two options give me the cash or get someone else to get the money for you. Now what is it going to be?" The man stammered and stuttered a bit then agreed to borrow money from a friend there at the sale. He gave the money to Herb and left the hall.

***

It was August 4th, 1972, nine years to the day from the opening of the Auction Barn and oh how the time had flown by. I would see my brothers and sisters at the auctions or on the job sites to talk and reminisce from time to time. I had not seen Sylvia for a spell and was curious how she was doing. I had heard rumors about her and her children having trouble with her husband. I was called by Maxine, to let me know that Sylvia had died the night before and was not sure of all the circumstances.

Sylvia was only 32 and the mother of four sons and two daughters. The oldest, Johnny Cake, being only 10 years old and a daughter Betty, only 8 at the time. Both were children from her first marriage to Joe Phinney. She had four other children while being married to Joe Latush. One of them being a son, Joey. She was a very hard worker and lived a lot in very sub poverty living conditions. She had a heart of gold and would give you the shirt off her back. I was bewildered and could not wait to talk to someone who really knew what had happened. I could only get bits and pieces from Dad and the rest of the family who were like me, going on hearsay or even speculation.

Or possibly they knew more than they wanted anyone else to know. It seems Sylvia was working at Gold Meadows, a nursing home in Danbury, when she was picked up by her husband, Joe and her son, Joey. They were all in the truck on their way home on Route 4, when she jumped from the truck and was killed instantly when she hit the pavement. There was testimony from Joe that he and she were having a heated conversation about her wanting to stop at someone's house on the way home. And when he refused to do that, Sylvia became enraged, opened the door and jumped to her death, leaving Joey in the truck. And then other sources of information tell a very different story.

For months prior to this incident there were charges of infidelity by Joe. He had been caught in bed with Sylvia's young daughter, Betty, by my brother, Art.

Art, on an unexpected visit to Sylvia's house, had entered unannounced. After a confrontation with Joe he went to Maxine's home where he shared the details of the event with her. Maxine became very enraged and called the police. As a result Joe was being investigated for molesting a minor.

There was a funeral and Sylvia's body was laid to rest in Plymouth River Side Cemetery. There were many people there, some I did not even know. In my heart I knew she was in a better place. However, I only regret that she could not have had a long and happy life.

At this funeral there were words of much anger from her first husband and the father of her two children, John and Betty. He vowed to get the bastard if it were the last thing he did in his life. He had heard rumors of physical and verbal abuse and promised that he was going to square things once and for all.

There were other threats which should have not been taken lightly. A friend at the auction stated if it were his sister, he would be castrated and gutted like an animal. And Eric, another friend, said, "I would knock him out and place him on a round oak table with his testicles hanging through the top where the expansion leaf goes. Then I would close it tight and pour gasoline around the table, wake him up and hand him a knife. Then I would step back and flick in a burning match." It was an imaginative source of vengeance, but not nearly as practical as other ones floating around.

At the auction that Saturday evening, there was conversation with the sheriff who was the investigating officer at the accident sight. He told Dad that Joe was going to be doing a couple of years for child abuse and Dad's comeback was, "He best stay there, that is the safest place for that son of a bitch."

It was a while before things got back to normal. I had been elected back into office and was also a member of the school board and sitting on the planning board. My children would go to the meetings and use the playground as the meetings were at the school.

The construction business had slowed to a point where I maintained only a couple small crews now. Building small chalets and remodeling was the main part of my construction.

Ever so often, I would hear rumors of how friends and relatives were still talking about Sylvia and her husband. There was a story about how a large wrench was found behind the seat of Joe's truck and and it contained blood and traces of hair, indicating that it was used to bludgeon Sylvia with. This added to the suspicion that he was the killer and he was soon to be released from prison.

"Whether he knows it or not, his f**kin' days are numbered." "If he does not die, he will only wished he had." And descriptive ideas on how he should be tortured were talked about at the auctions most every week. Some were just showing their sympathy and others thought that the investigation was not as good as it should have been. I thought that it was just a lot of talk.

And for Joe Latush, his time in the pen was up and he was eventually released from prison. He got a job and was working on a logging crew nearby. It was not long before he was found in the woods there, seriously injured from a blow to the head. He was taken by ambulance to a hospital nearby where he soon died. There was a lot of talk as to what had really happened. I had been told many stories to do with

Sylvia and Joe's death and I can only take what evidence I know to be true and speculate on the real cause of his demise. At the auction, Dad was informed of the particulars by Sheriff Ash, who was the investigating officer. Dad was very passive and showed no interest, as though he already knew more than the Sheriff. So Herb said, "For the record, I've already ruled it an accident." And it was left like that, oh the talking went on for a while after that, but it did go away.

I ran the auctions here and other places for another ten years or more. Always searching for the better mouse trap, but using the public with honesty and fairness.

Most of my life I have entertained guests, my children, relatives and friends by sharing experiences from my past and people appear to appreciate them. I am going on seventy four now and looking back sometimes looks like a long road. The journey has not been one without some very heart wrenching events, however my troubled childhood did produce some moments of pure unadulterated happiness and I do not take them lightly. I, like so many people, am a product of my environment. I learned from my mother, her mother, my father, and so many other people who have shared my life. I guess that is what is referred to as the School Of Hard Knocks. I have remained a student of this institution my entire life and believe that if a day should pass without learning something, a day of your short life has been wasted. My mother was also a product of her environment and even though she lived a very short life, she had learned from her mother and the other people in her life. She taught me to walk, talk, stand straight and tall and all the basics that all young people should know, but she also taught me the importance of hygiene, presence and appearance. The value of looking great. The value of knowledge and many things so necessary to life. Most of all from her I learned to save for rainy days and how to live with the bare essentials. There are so many basic things I learned in life from people around me, not all good, but I have learned to recognize good from bad. However, I, like so many others, have made mistakes and that is how we learn. I believe, it is important to decide just what one wants out of life here on earth. Then become prepared and do what it takes to be the best at that. If that takes formal education, then I believe one should pursue the best possible.

Mom was with me for only 15 years before her death, and that time was interrupted when I chose to stay with other people. However, I believe she had a more profound impression on me than anyone else in my past 73 years and she still visits me frequently in the night to console and advise me. Oh there was Dad, Grammy, Grandpa, my siblings, Chet Lawson and so many others, but a big part of my life was so influenced by her that there are a very few days that can pass without me thinking about it in one way or another. I could have never survived in the back woods of Wisconsin that winter of 1955, saved and invested for a rainy day or lived the life which I did, if I had not listened to her voice which is so implanted in my mind.

These are a few of her quotes she had passed on to me. I cannot say that I followed them as closely as I should have. However, they and many others, have influenced the way I live my life.

> "Stop and think about it before you do it or say it."
> "Don't do things to other people that you would not want done to you."
> "Hold your head high and stand or sit straight and tall."
> "Cleanliness is next to Godliness."
> "Make sure you sow only the seeds that you wish to reap."
> "Look out for your pennies and the dollars will look out for themselves."
> "If you do not have anything good to say about someone, then do not say anything."
> "If you are wishing for a loaf of bread, you may as well wish for the whole grocery store. It costs no more."
> "A dollar saved is a dollar earned."
> "Life is not cast in concrete, you have the power to change it."
> "Make up your mind what you want out of life and work toward that goal, do not get side tracked."

My brother, George was suffering from cancer at his home in Dorchester. I went to visit him a few times and could see that he was failing fast. He passed away October 6, 1979.

I was married to Patricia for 24 years trying to make a ago of it. We had five children: Jerry, Chris, Tate, Victoria and Jeff. There were many times of adventure and happiness, but the bad just out-weighed the good. So, as to stop the torturing of each other, we agreed to separate. The children were pretty much out of the house and they encouraged me to make the move. So in 1982, Patricia and I were divorced.

My firstborn, Jerry, passed away at age 24 from cancer In October of the next fall.

I married Wendy Williams January of 1983. We had common interests and I loved being a part of her life.

My second son, Chris, died after 12 years struggling with HIV in 1995.

In the spring of 1988, while I was working in the Virgin Islands, Dad passed away.

In the fall of 2001 while at a family reunion I met a new brother, Leslie, who is "my brother from another mother".

In February of 2008, Maxine passed away from cancer and liver complications.

In all, now I have four brothers, one sister and a half brother. They are still working at the trades they had learned from Dad and Mom. They, their children, and grandchildren are living in New Hampshire near where they were born.

Wendy and I have been married now for nearly 30 years. We have an artist son, Ty, 27 in LA, California and a daughter, Reese, 22 in Kittery, Maine.

My family has had both good and bad luck. However, most are following the path of their parents and reluctant to getting out of the rut made earlier by their family.

I have lived to see many changes in things during my life, thirteen different presidents, the communication and information explosion, from mail service to computers and cell phones and medical marvels.

People now live longer, but a lot of them are a product of their environment. People sound, look and act like their parents.

I ran auctions for many years and enjoyed the trade a lot. I also had my own real estate office and construction business for a long time, all of which I enjoyed. I still build houses and toy with other trades to help anyone I can.

Made in the USA
Middletown, DE
30 July 2024